The Root Of Shame
The Deal we make with Evil

by John Byron Shank

Peniel Publishing
All Rights Reserved

All Bible quotes are from the ESV translation unless otherwise stated.

Acknowledgements
I would like to thank the following for their help and
encouragement in editing, feedback, and support in
writing this book: Bob and Sarah Hazen, Karen Reipe,
and the Staff and students at Metro Hope, Minneapolis MN.

Special thanks to the Root of Shame class members who helped
me so much in clarifying what needed to be said, and doing the
hard work of this inventory.

All opinions and conclusions in this book are mine, unless otherwise credited.

The Author
At this writing, I am a Pastoral Counselor and Teacher at Metro
Hope, a Bible based addiction in-patient rehab facility in Minneapolis, Minnesota. This book is the text for a class called **The Root
of Shame.**

I also teach other classes for men at the Ramsey County Jail in St.
Paul, Minnesota, addressing issues regarding reconnection of fa-
thers to their families. The men's parenting class is called:
Recovering My Moral Integrity As A Father.

This book is dedicated to:
those who have harmed me, and those whom I have harmed.

Foreword   1

How To Use This Book   7
Root of Shame Member Agreement   9
The Shame Inventory Chart   12

Chapter 1. The Root of Shame   14
The Vine Psalm   14
The Power of Sin   18
Satan infects my mental process with bad code   22
Condemnation Vs. Conviction   27
Shame Sources   30
Shame Chart   34

Chapter 2. Sharper Than a Two-edged Sword   36
Body, Soul & Spirit Diagram   40
House Cleaning Prayer   43
A Definition of the Soul   45
The Soul and the Addiction Cycle   48
Healing and Brain Training   51

Chapter 3. True and False Affections   55
Deals and Plays   56
Infatuation   59
The Power of Procreation   60
Sexual Shame   61
The Strong Shame the Weak   62

Chapter 4. Wrong Believing   66
Faith Chart   68
Rhema and The Faith Process   69
The Opiate of Passivity   72

The Progress of Corruption   72
Logos and Rhema   75

Chapter 5. Right Believing   **78**
Reckoning   80
The Word that does not lie   82
The Truth About Me   86
The Truth About God   89

Chapter 6. In Summary   **94**
Process chains, set-ups and scripts   96
Trigger› Interpreter› Conceit› False payoff›
True Payoff› Consequences   99
Trigger Loops & Loop Breakers   103
Trigger Loops In Response to Fear   104
Various Trigger Loop Examples   106
How to make a Trigger Loop   111
Trigger Loop Worksheets   116

Chapter 7. Sabotage   **119**
Games & Conceits   120
Repentance   123
Sabotage, Narcissism, & Contempt   127
Contempt breeds narcissism   128

Chapter 8. The forgiveness Process   **130**
Break the power of others to take away your
peace and value   134
How does the death of Jesus pay for my sins?   137
How does the death of Christ break the power
of Satan?   139
Forgiveness Prayer   140

Chapter 9.   Making Amends   144
Bloodguilt on the Land   149
A Guide for Making Amends   152
Showing Throat   153
Amends in Spiritual Intercession   156

Chapter 10.The Maintenance of Relationship   162
True Self Versus False Self   163
Overcoming vs. Being Overthrown   168
The Freedoms   174

Epilogue   178
A Guide To Discussion Group Leaders   178
One-To-One Follow Ups   181

Bibliography   186

My Beginning

I Corinthians 13:11-12 says:

> When I was a child, I spoke as a child, I thought like a child, I reasoned like a child. When I became a man, I gave up childish ways. For now we see in a mirror dimly, but then face to Face. Now I know in part; then I shall know fully, even as I am fully known. – ESV

It is amazing how many conclusions I came to, and how many foundational assumptions I never challenged—that were formed when I was still a child without mature understanding. In my self-examination, I only saw myself dimly, in part because what I was looking at was false. There were other things I did not *want* to see because that would mean making changes I was *not willing* to make. So my motives were also false. But conviction by the Holy Spirit has prevailed in me to have courage to look into the brightness of the Word.

My friend, *Brian Coatney*, says in his devotional book, *A YEAR IN WHO WE ARE*, for July 23, referring to the bias of the soul in ourselves:

> "Nothing about the self tells us who we are because self cannot be its own mirror... Sensing incompleteness, the self looks to others as mirrors since God created man to need approval. However, until God is known as the mirror, others take His place."

Proverbs 1:20-23 says:

> Wisdom cries aloud in the street, in the markets she raises her voice;

at the head of the noisy streets she cries out;
at the entrance of the noisy gates she speaks:
"How long, O simple ones, will you love being simple?
How long will scoffers delight in their scoffing and fools
    hate knowledge?
If you turn at my reproof, behold, I will pour out my spirit
    to you;
I will make my words known to you. – ESV

I deceived myself when I wanted to remain unable to see the truth in some areas of my life where I still had sinful agendas, or where I had no faith or will to overcome. But addictive and controlling behavior patterns were keeping me from healthy relationships. Self-loathing stood in the place of humility. Instead of zeal I had anger. Complaining about my violated rights took the place of gratitude. Truth was suppressed so I could believe what I *wanted* to be true, to justify my sin. Pride stood in the place meant for healthy dignity. A hard heart prevented me from having a kinder one. When I finally started to take a serious look at my life, I thought my root problem was bitterness. Now I see my root problem had been unresolved shame. What follows is what I have learned to help heal a life that has been crippled by the root of shame.

I hate to be ashamed. I have tried to minimize it, or blame others, or make excuses to justify myself, or I have tried to medicate it. Some try to say the problem is God's Law—and so become lawless libertines who let no one tell them what to do, and pay no attention to the effect their sins have on others. But the only solution is to face shame head-on by dealing with God honestly. Without God's Law there can be no Justice. Without God's grace there is no way to begin again. Without the Holy Spirit there is no deep repentance. Without the sacrifice of Christ there is no hope.

The inventories in this book are designed to develop skills in becoming systematic in my repentance. This is because there are systems of sin inside me—Satan, through the willing cooperation of my flesh, created set-ups in my soul's reasoning that gave me permission to sin. The world recognizes some of these sin systems too, though they would call them disorders, like narcissism for example.

Narcissistic behaviors include grandiosity, arrogance, being exploitive, being entitled for special preference over others, envious, and lacking empathy for their victims. Many of these traits show up in **Romans 1:28-32** which says:

> And since they did not see fit to acknowledge God, God gave them up to a debased mind to do what ought not to be done. They were filled with all manner of unrighteousness, evil, covetousness, malice. They are full of envy, murder, strife, deceit, maliciousness. They are gossips, slanderers, haters of God, insolent, haughty, boastful, inventors of evil, disobedient to parents, foolish, faithless, heartless, ruthless. Though they know God's righteous decree that those who practice such things deserve to die, they not only do them but give approval to those who practice them. — ESV

This does not mean all mental and emotional disorders are caused by sin. But sin systems are usually embedded with guilt that powerfully impact our mental and emotional state. The enemy was able to use my unchallenged sin systems to construct a false identity in me—that I was stuck on stupid and stuck on sick. My sin systems created corruptions in my behavior, distortions in my thinking and perversions in my believing about God.

A ditty on the situation in **Romans 7:15** goes:
> When I do the don'ts, and I don't do the do's.
> I don't understand why I choose what I do.

But it is very important that I learn to understand what is going on with my choices. This means more than just confessing sin when it happens. If I am a new creation in Christ by the indwelling of the Holy Spirit, how does the evil one still fool me? What deals with the devil still remain in my thinking that give me permission to sin? What misbeliefs still hijack my faith? What sinful vows and covenants do I still harbor, and why? (For example: I will NEVER again let anyone get that close... I am so DONE with her...) Why do I still relapse into old behavior that Christ-in-me hates? By the Spirit I am clean, but my soul needs to be healed. In Satan, my sin was personalized as me. Now in Christ, His righteousness must be personalized as the real me, as I stand on what His Word says is now true about me, and begin to learn His new ways.

Fear of judgment produces shame, but by hiding my guilt with rationalizations I bring harm to my conscience. Born again believers have a new purified spirit identity, but sin still opposes my spirit through my flesh. I have changed the pronouns in the following verse from the plural (we and us) to first person singular (I and me) to personalize the force of the meaning. As Scripture shows us in **Galatians 5:17**:
> For the desires of *my* flesh are against the Spirit [in my human spirit], and the desires of the Spirit are against *my* flesh,

for these are opposed to each other to keep *me* from doing what *I* want to do. - ESV [Shank]

So, who is the *real me* that wants to do something? Is it who I am in my new spirit indwelt by the Spirit of God—expressing Christ in obedience through my form? Or is it who I may still believe I am according to the desires of my flesh—in disobedience expressing evil through my form? Praise God, His Spirit sparks the desire for moral integrity.

John 12:23-27 says:

> And Jesus answered them, "The hour has come for the Son of Man to be glorified. Truly, truly, I say to you, unless a grain of wheat falls into the earth and dies, it remains alone; but if it dies, it bears much fruit. Whoever loves his life loses it, and whoever hates his life in this world will keep it for eternal life. If anyone serves Me, he must follow Me; and where I am, there will My servant be also. If anyone serves Me, the Father will honor him.

> Now My soul is troubled. And what shall I say? 'Father save Me from this hour'? But for this purpose I have come to this hour." - ESV

In order for Christ to be fully manifest through me, my old fleshly ways of living must die—like the wheat seed—in order to bear fruit. Is my soul troubled at this? Yes. Jesus had to die for us, and was His soul troubled at this? Yes. But He obeyed His Father and did His Father's will. Jesus was tempted in every way common to man. This means He experienced spirit vs. flesh conflict in temptation.

John 12:25 says:
> Whoever loves his life will lose it, and whoever hates his life in this world will keep it for eternal life. - ESV

I must hate the sin in the life I still live in the flesh, because if I do, I will seek my Father for wisdom to overcome by the Spirit of Christ in my spirit. This is troubling to my soul which may be afraid to face the painful truth about the deals I have made with evil that may still remain to sabotage my thinking. **Question**: Since my sins are under the Blood, why should I look back at them? **Answer**: So I will bear more fruit by learning how to remove any lies that still remain—and break the power of Shame.

John 12 :35-36
> So Jesus said to them, "The Light is among you for a little while longer. Walk while you have the Light, lest darkness overtake you. The one who walks in the darkness does not know where he is going. While you have the Light, believe in the Light, that you may become sons of the Light. - ESV

So with courage, go forth with these inventories that you may walk in the Light so that the darkness will no longer overtake you.

Luke 3:4-6 says:
> As it is written in the book of the words of Isaiah the prophet, "The voice of one crying in the wilderness: 'Prepare the way of the Lord, make his paths straight. [be honest about what is going on] Every valley shall be filled, [not giving in to despair or pessimism] and every mountain and hill shall be made low, [not being proud or grandiose] and the crooked shall become straight, [not manipulative,

lying, or deviant] and the rough places shall become level ways, [not being inconsistent or double minded] and all flesh shall see the salvation of God.'" – ESV [Shank]

How To Use This Book

This book is designed to be used privately, with a close friend, or in small group sessions.

If you are doing these inventories by yourself, having someone you trust give feedback at certain points, can be very constructive. The God who loves you knows what was done to you and what you did to others. If you are born again in Christ, you are already forgiven. Jesus said; "Blessed are they that mourn, for they shall be comforted." It is a holy thing to confront your own unholiness.

There is a chart at the end of this introduction you can blow up on a copy machine as large as you can. I make them 11 x 17 inches. Or you could draw one yourself. Make three or four copies for yourself or per person in the group, so each has plenty of room to list examples.

You can also download a free 11 x 17 worksheet from: johnbyronshank.com/Books/Free Downloads/The Shame Inventory Worksheet/Get it

When you do **Column 1**, just name a specific *incident* that happened that triggers you when you remember it. Just write a phrase in the box as a reference. There is no need to write the whole story out. We know how we were hurt, or what we did to hurt someone else. In **Column 1** you may say only **Joe after the party.** (for your shameful memory) In **Column 2** (How was I hurt?) you might say:

He betrayed me. Later in the process **Column 4** you might say: **so I spread nasty rumors about him and keyed his car.** Get the idea? Each chapter of the book will direct you in how to do each column.

It is important to keep your charts in a safe place where no one else can read them so you can be fearlessly honest about what you write. You don't want to block the discovery of a real insight because you minimized or exaggerated parts of the story, either. If the facts of a problem are not revealed on the paper, the real answers will not show up either. Your problems are in reality. God is in reality. If there is an answer—it will Only be found in reality where the truth is—where the Lord is.

In a group setting, it may be a good idea to have all participants read the agreement which follows—and sign each other's copies of this book—to protect the confidences of one another. I also recommend that group members be all of the same gender since sexual wounds carry a lot of shame, and the truth may not be fully addressed in mixed company.

Also, in a group setting, I never ask the participants to read their 30-40 shame examples to the class. There is no need to make someone shame themselves in front of others. That would seriously undermine the productivity of the deep internal honesty the inventories require. But as trust in the group is built, we will need feedback on significant situations. The group is encouraged to volunteer patterns and insights in meetings as we go forward, in order to get feedback or to pass on encouragement. All must participate by sharing something real. There is no growth without stretching and real change is often outside my comfort zone. My secrets can keep me sick. Besetting sins and addictions are built on the same old familiar assumptions and beliefs that have been assumed to be normal and never challenged.

Root of Shame Group Member Agreement (this is a modified version of the Redemption Group Participation Agreement for Mike Wilkerson's book *Redemption*.)

I agree to the following in my group:

Attendance: Except for unavoidable circumstances, I will attend all planned group sessions.

Homework: I will read the assigned chapter and come prepared to share, with written answers to the questions for each lesson.

Privacy: I will respect the privacy of other group members by not sharing their personal details outside the group. I understand that my leader may consult with other counselors for advice or prayer on my behalf. Details will be held in confidence between them.

Sharing my experience: I will share what I learn about myself in this group. I am free to share my experience about myself outside the group so long as I protect the confidentiality of the other group members.

No intoxication: I will not attend classes under the influence of any intoxication from drugs or alcohol.

Distractions: I will be mindful of the dignity of on-going discussion by not engaging in side conversations, cell phone use, or getting up and walking out of the room, et cetera.

Respect: I will not speak profanely to others, minimize their pain, trivialize their problems with simplistic advice, or speak harshly.

Full participation: I understand that I am not here for myself alone, but as a group member I will commit to actively love my fellow members by showing compassion, encouraging, asking relevant questions, and confronting graciously. I understand that sometimes I can participate best by not talking all the time to give others a chance to contribute to the discussion.

Healthy discomfort: I understand that there will be times of healthy discomfort in this group because sin and suffering can be hard to face. I will accept the Holy Spirit's role as Comforter in the group, and will avoid coddling or rescuing others with touching, out of my own feelings of discomfort.

Speaking up in the group: I understand that the group meeting is the best time to speak up. I will risk speaking my mind in the group and will not reserve my thoughts for private conversations with leadership. When relevant conversation does occur outside the group, I will bring it back to the group.

Conflict engagement: I understand that when healthy conflict occurs, the Holy Spirit will use it for the good of all, so I will remain engaged even if I am the one being challenged. I will take responsibility for my own thoughts and actions when I challenge someone else. I will avoid fruitless arguments about irrelevant matters.

Foreword

Please print your name below with the date.

_____

_____

_____

_____

_____

_____

_____

THE SHAME INVENTORY (The Root of Shame / John Byron Shank / Peniel Publishing)

MY SHAMEFUL MEMORIES	HOW WAS I HURT?	HOW DID I HURT OTHERS?	HOW DID I GET REVENGE OR CONSOLE MYSELF?	WHAT DID I WRONGLY BELIEVE ABOUT ME?	HOW WAS GOD'S TRUTH CORRUPTED?	WHAT IS THE BIBLICAL TRUTH?
Column 1	Column 2	Column 3	Column 4	Column 5	Column 6	Column 7
1						
2						
3						
4						
5						
6						
7						
8						
9						
0						

Foreword

1

The Root of Shame

*Lord, give me the courage to face the truth about what You have
already forgiven in me.*

The Vine
When I was sixteen
I wanted to ditch myself
Down by the side of the road,
Leave myself behind by the side of the road.
Tried on so many other faces
But I never could find one that I could call my own.
Tried on so many other faces
But I never could find one that I could call my own.

There was a twig at the end
Of a long spreading branch
That was my family tree,
And I knew that twig was me.
I thought no matter how hard I try

There was nobody else that I could be.
I thought no matter how hard I try
There was nobody else that I could be.

But there's a knowledge that comes
In the delay of an answer
And a wisdom that comes,
Comes in the delay of relief,
And a truth that can be heard while waiting in the silence
For that still, small Voice to speak.
Yes, a truth that can be heard while waiting in the silence
For that still, small Voice to speak.

The Words of the Lord are flawless
Like silver refined in a furnace of clay
Purified seven times,
Refined in a furnace seven times.
They say my life is in the Vine,
My spirit is His and His Spirit is mine.
They say my life is in the Vine,
My spirit is His and His Spirit is mine.
– *River of Delights* / Peniel Music / johnbyronshank.com

Is shame good or evil? The answer is that it depends on how we respond to it. Some of us are tortured by it. Others of us seem to have no shame at all. For those of us who experience a lot of it, shame is self-loathing with fear of exposure—I am damaged goods, or a wrong person. It can be the result of an offense to my body or my vanity, or dignity, by someone else. It can also be caused by my own ruthlessly sinful behaviors toward another.

If I feel no shame for what I have done, I must take heed. It might be because I can no longer feel the effects of my sins on others because

I have suppressed my conscience and hardened my heart. In the worst case scenario, **Jeremiah 8:12** says:

> Were they ashamed when they committed abomination?
> No, they were not at all ashamed;
> they did not know how to blush.
> Therefore they shall fall among the fallen;
> when I punish them, they shall be overthrown,
> says the Lord. – ESV

Shame is not the problem. What has been done *by me* to others, or what others have done *to me* to make me feel ashamed, is the real problem. But, if the causes for my shame are not addressed, shame goes toxic and warps my ability to perceive what is truly happening around me. It will also cause serious erosion in my capacity to believe rightly about God or myself.

- Your sin has betrayed the shalom of God in me.
- My sin has betrayed the shalom of God in you.
- My sin also damages the shalom of God in me.

Shalom means peace. Creation itself came out of the shalom of God. In paradise, shalom will be fully restored. Violation of that peace is a deep wounding, which is often hidden by emotional blocking, or with secrets to avoid painful exposure. It plays a major part in the avoidance of God in prayer, in the fruitful expectation of faith, and in hindering intimate fellowship with others. Unbroken by repentance, self-loathing shame leads to downward spirals of thinking and behavior that make problems worse and worse. After Adam and Eve disobeyed God by eating from the Tree of the Knowledge of Good and Evil, they saw they were naked and covered themselves in shame.

Genesis 3:8-13 says:

> And they heard the sound of the Lord God walking in the garden in the cool of the day, and the man and his wife hid themselves from the presence of the Lord God among the trees of the garden. But the Lord God called to the man and said to him "Where are you?" And he said, "I heard the sound of You in the garden, and I was afraid, because I was naked, and hid myself." He [The Lord] said, "Who told you that you were naked? Have you eaten of the Tree of which I commanded you not to eat?" The man said, "The woman whom You gave to be with me, she gave me fruit of the tree, and I ate." Then the Lord God said to the woman, "What is this that you have done?" The woman said, "The serpent deceived me, and I ate." – ESV [Shank]

Notice that the disobedience of Adam and Eve made them see themselves as naked, as exposed in the painful light of Truth. Adam and Eve were ashamed in the presence of the Lord in the Garden of Eden. This made them try to hide from the All-seeing and All-knowing God Who made them. Christ, the Word of the Lord, called to the man, "Where are you?" not because He didn't know where they were, but because He wanted them to stand before Him in the Light and confess the truth with their own lips.

Adam's confession was cowardly and insulting because he blamed God by inference: "The woman whom You gave to be with me, she gave me fruit of the tree, and I ate." The implication here is that God had given him someone who was flawed to be his companion, so he was not entirely at fault for what he did. Never mind that he knew better and put her above the command of the Lord. Adam saw that he could have what she now had and be able to know what she now knew.

Eve rightly blamed Satan for deceiving her, but she did not acknowledge that she also became an instrument of corruption in drawing Adam into her sin. She wanted what Satan wanted—to grab more power by willful disobedience, which the Most High had withheld. She was quick to pull her husband into her sin. Jesus was not like that.

Philippians 2:5-8 says:

> Have this mind among yourselves, which is yours in Christ Jesus, Who, though He was in the form of God, did not count equality with God a thing to be grasped, but made Himself empty, by taking the form of a servant, being born in the likeness of men. And being found in human form, He humbled Himself by becoming obedient to the point of death, even death on a cross. – ESV

The Power of Sin

Ahab, the king of Israel was a wicked man. Nevertheless, God sent prophets to him in Samaria, to warn him about his sins, and to give him a chance to repent. The power of evil **had** Ahab, and the king of Syria came against him with all the ruthlessness of Satan himself.

1 Kings 20: 1-6 says:

> Ben-hadad the king of Syria gathered his army together. Thirty-two kings were with him, and horses and chariots. And he went up and closed in on Samaria and fought against it. And he sent messengers into the city to Ahab king of Israel and said to him, "Thus says Ben-hadad: Your silver and your gold are mine; your best wives and children are mine." And the king of Israel answered, "As you say, my lord O king, I am yours, and all that I have." The messengers came again

and said, "Thus says Ben-hadad: I sent to you, saying, "Deliver to me your silver and your gold, your wives and your children." Nevertheless, I will send my servants to you tomorrow about this time, and they will search your house and the houses of your servants and lay hands on whatever pleases you and take it away. – ESV

It is interesting that both the Hebrew words in the Old Testament and the Greek words in the New Testament for *messenger* can both also mean *angel*. Ben-hadad sending his messenger parallels the Devil sending one of his *messengers* or *angels*, which are *demons*. Those of us who have been addicted know what it is like to be ruled over by a ruthless spirit who will take everything we love from us. Those of us who have been filled with pride, violence, abusiveness, lust and fear know that spirit too. See Ahab's admission to Ben-hadad, "As you say, my lord O king, I am yours, and all that I have." (my silver and gold, my wives and children.)

Why would Ahab say that? Why would he agree to hand over his family and his wealth? It was because he was surrounded by a great army. He could not defeat them in battle, or flee for help. He was trapped. He had to do what was demanded of him. It is the same for those of us who have become enslaved to addiction. Our very will and dignity are taken away. We are hopeless. Surely the devil has power over us, he does whatever he pleases with us. How can we ever break loose from his sinful and destructive demands? We have always failed at our best efforts. How can we come to *believe in*, and even *know* a God Who is loving and strong, and willing to free us? The devil has power over us in our sin and can only be defeated by One Who is more powerful than he is. Only the One Who is Powerful in Righteousness can make us righteous.

The Greek word for sin is **harmartia**, which literally means to miss the mark, as in missing a target in archery. But the Bible does not say that those who will be sent to Hell are there because they are poor archers. Those in Hell are there because they refused to repent by exchanging their sin operator (Satan) for the righteous Operator (Christ). The Greek word for operator is **energeo**. We produce the works of the master we obey—by his power (**energeo**) through us. Only Christ or Satan can act as our moral energizer, our moral operator. We will love one and hate the other.

According to W.E. Vine in his *Expository Dictionary of New Testament Words*, sin is described as "a principle source of action, or an inward element producing acts." Vine also refers to sin as "a governing principle or power," citing **Romans 6:6** where sin is here spoken of as an organized power, acting through the members of the body. Satan is acting as my sin operator.

Romans 6:6 says:
> We know that our old self was crucified with Him in order that the body of sin might be brought to nothing, so that we would no longer be enslaved to sin. - ESV

Romans 7:8,11 says:
> But sin, seizing an opportunity through the commandment, produced in me all kinds of covetousness.
>
> For sin, seizing an opportunity through the commandment, deceived me and through it killed me. - ESV

If the Bible says my old self (old spirit nature) was crucified with Christ—put to death in Him, why do I still sin, if I am born again? The answer is that while my old sinful nature is now dead, sin still finds access to me through the weakness of my flesh. Sin seizes opportunity through the weakness of my flesh (Greek **sarx**). Satan is Mr. Sin. So, how does Satan do that?

Romans 7:15-20 says:

> For I do not understand my own actions. For I do not do what I want, but I do the very thing I hate. Now if I do what I do not want, I agree with the law that it is good. So now it is no longer I who do it, but sin that dwells within me. For I know that nothing good dwells in me, that is my flesh (**sarx**). For I have the desire to do what is right, but not the ability to carry it out. For I do not do the good I want, but the evil I do not want is what I keep on doing. Now if I do what I do not want, *it is no longer I that do it*, but sin that dwells within me. – ESV

Galatians 5:17 says:

> For the desires of flesh are against the Spirit, and the desires of the Spirit are against the flesh, for these are opposed to each other, to keep you from doing the things you want to do. – ESV

Question. How is it that a believer, whose human spirit is regenerated by the presence of the Holy Spirit, can still have sin in his members—in his flesh?

Answer. I believe that my fears and anxieties from past wounds, to me from others, or by me to others, harbor doubt and shame in my soul. Are fear and anxiety sin? No, not in and of themselves. But temptation appeals to whatever is swarming in my mental and emotional reservoir that has not been resolved by faith. It takes advantage of unconfessed sin, unforgiveness, painful recall, a

21

blocked conscience, a weak will, and a heart that has not been regularly cleansed by the Blood. There is real pain and real vulnerability about these things.

In examining my own ways and the ways of others whom I have observed, I have also come to see a process which may prove to be useful. The mind that God has given us is marvelous. Not only is it a great storehouse of memories, thoughts, and powers of reasoning, it is also able to learn reflexive responses we routinely rely on as habits. Those habits become automatic responses—like pathways—reinforced through repetition. What do I do when I feel threatened, or lonely, or attracted to someone, et cetera? I respond out of my habits.

My habits of response were designed to serve as a way to conserve brain energy by collapsing my thinking into a quick shortcut, so I can preserve time and brain energy needed to solve more complex problems. This is a good thing to be able to do because it creates a mental efficiency which allows me to manage and prioritize my efforts. But the capacity I have for habitual response to similar provocations is actively undermined by lying assumptions planted in my mind and heart by the evil one, through the weakness of my flesh.

Satan infects my mental process with bad code.

The Scripture says that Satan's name was Lucifer before he was cast out of heaven. His original name means *Light-bearer*, and he must have had an original purpose in bringing light to the souls of mankind. He was originally given access to the mind, emotions and imagination of men and women. But now, instead of being an illuminator, his name is changed to Satan, the *Deceiver*. He corrupts my soul's ability to see or rightly understand what is happening around me. He influences my mood. He injects bad code: thoughts and false conclusions to affect my heart's desires—to bend my will towards his ends.

Ezekiel 28:11-19 says Lucifer was originally "the signet [brightest example] of perfection, blameless in his ways, an anointed guardian cherub," where he saw the Face of God Who had placed him on the holy mountain of God. But with no excuse, he rebelled against the God Whose goodness he knew Face to face and for his defiance he was cast down.

In **Ezekiel 28:1-10** says:

> The word of the Lord came to me: "Son of man, say to the **prince** of Tyre, Thus says the Lord God:
>
> "Because your heart is proud,
> and you have said, 'I am a god,
> I sit in the seat of the gods,
> in the heart of the seas,'
> yet you are but a man, and no god,
> though you make your heart like the heart of a god—
> you are indeed wiser than Daniel;
> no secret is hidden from you; by your wisdom and your understanding
> you have made wealth for yourself,
> and have gathered gold and silver
> into your treasuries;
> by your great wisdom in your trade (deals)
> you have increased your wealth,
> and your heart has become proud in your wealth—
> therefore thus says the Lord God:
> Because you make your heart

like the heart of a god,
therefore, behold, I will bring foreigners upon you,
the most ruthless of the nations;
and they shall draw their swords against the beauty of your
wisdom and defile your splendor.
They shall thrust you down into the pit,
and you shall die the death of the slain
in the heart of the seas.
Will you still say, 'I am a god,'
in the presence of those who kill you,
though you are but a man, and no god,
in the hands of those who slay you?
You shall die the death of the uncircumcised
by the hand of foreigners;
for I have spoken, declares the Lord God." –ESV (*Shank*)

And **Ezekiel 28:11-19** says:

Moreover, the word of the Lord came to me: "Son of
man, raise a lamentation over the **king** of Tyre, and say to
him, Thus says the Lord God:

"You were the signet of perfection,
full of wisdom and perfect in beauty.
You were in Eden, the garden of God;
every precious stone was your covering,
sardius, topaz, and diamond,
beryl, onyx, and jasper,
sapphire, emerald, and carbuncle;
and crafted in gold were your settings
and your engravings.
On the day that you were created
they were prepared.

24

You were an anointed guardian cherub.
I placed you; you were on the holy mountain of God;
in the midst of the stones of fire you walked.
You were blameless in your ways
from the day you were created,
till unrighteousness was found in you.
In the abundance of your trade
you were filled with violence in your midst, and you
sinned;
so I cast you as a profane thing from the mountain of God,
and I destroyed you, O guardian cherub,
from the midst of the stones of fire.
Your heart was proud because of your beauty;
you corrupted your wisdom for the sake of your splendor.
I cast you to the ground;
I exposed you before kings,
to feast their eyes on you.
By the multitude of your iniquities,
in the unrighteousness of your trade (sin deals)
you profaned your sanctuaries;
so I brought fire out from your midst;
it consumed you,
and I turned you to ashes on the earth
in the sight of all who saw you.
All who know you among the peoples
are appalled at you;
you have come to a dreadful end
and shall be no more forever." – ESV (Shank)

In **Ezekiel 28:1-19**, the **prince** of Tyre is described in all his selfish arrogance. But when the **king** of Tyre is described, we can see that he is not a man, but an angel (spirit master) who manifests his evil nature through the prince of Tyre (his vessel), a man who was a slave to reproducing the devil's will. I believe the reason the prince of Tyre is compared to the king of Tyre in this passage, is to show the relationship between the root and branch, father and son—the devil's evil being expressed in those who are his.

Isaiah 14:12-17

> "How you are fallen from heaven,
> O Day Star, son of Dawn!
> How you are cut down to the ground,
> you who laid the nations low!
> You said in your heart,
> I will ascend to heaven;
> above the stars of God
> I will set my throne on high;
> I will sit on the mount of assembly
> in the far reaches of the north;
> I will ascend above the heights of the clouds;
> I will make myself like the Most High.'
> But you are brought down to Sheol,
> to the far reaches of the pit.
> Those who see you will stare at you
> and ponder over you:
> 'Is this the man who made the earth tremble,
> who shook kingdoms,
> who made the world like a desert
> and overthrew its cities,
> who did not let his prisoners go home?' - ESV

This passage describes the fall of the illuminator, Lucifer. **Isaiah 14:4** compares him to the king of Babylon, who also expresses Satan's evil nature. Though thrown out of heaven, the devil (slanderer) knows the way into you and me by subverting the self-interest focus of my soul and the weakness of my flesh. Once an intended Illuminator, he has now become the Deceiver.

The beast in **Revelation 13** is given power by the devil. The beast is a man, the antichrist, who will oppress the whole world after the Holy Spirit is taken out of the world by the rapture of the real church (**2 Thessalonians 2:7-8**). But in my own history, has the devil sometimes been able to make a beast of me? A beast of bitterness? A beast of rage? A beast of fear? A beast of lust or pride? A beast of ruthlessness? A beast of control or manipulation? Not seeing my beast keeps me from seeing my desperate need for Jesus.

Condemnation Versus Conviction

Condemnation is different than conviction. Condemnation affects the value of who I *am*—conviction condemns what I have *done*. Satan takes advantage of me when I sin, by using the Law against me for condemnation. He wants me to hate myself to the point of despair. He is *Notgod* the *Unmaker* and wants to draw me into morbid shame if he can, to make me believe I am hopeless.

Jesus says that he who hates his life will keep it, and he who loses his life will find it. The Lord also says that I should agree with my accuser on the way to the judge, so the judge may not condemn me (**Matthew 5:25**). If Satan is my accuser, under what circumstances can I agree with him? (My sins *yes*, his conclusions about what it means *no*, if I am now in Christ.) Jesus also says to the Pharisees, "Your accuser is Moses" (**John 5:45**).

Romans 7:12 says:
>So, the Law is holy, and the commandment is holy and righteous and good. – ESV

Ironically, both Moses and Satan use the Law against us: Satan to *condemn* us for sin; but Moses to *convict* us of sin.

Romans 8:1-2 says:
> There is therefore now no condemnation for those who are in Christ Jesus. For the Law of the Spirit of life has set me free in Christ Jesus from the Law of sin and death. – ESV

So, what conclusions should we draw? Let's review the difference between condemnation and conviction. When I sin, Satan condemns me saying, "You're worthless, you're hopelessly corrupt, you can't do right, just give up!" But the Holy Spirit convicts me saying, "Why did you do *that?* You're better than *that*, you're a child of God, get back on track!" The Holy Spirit actually affirms me by saying the *thing I did* was wrong. "Sin is no longer your master. Make it right; repent because in Christ you have a nature like Christ." To the Christian, condemnation is *never* from the Holy Spirit. I'm learning to reject condemnation in Jesus' Name and to agree with the conviction of whoever is right in accusing me of sin.

I just need to confess, change, and move on in faith. Regarding shame, it's important to realize that the enemy may be right in pointing out that what I did was wrong or even terrible, but my acknowledgement of my sin does not mean I must also take on his condemning conclusion about who I am. I must reject that condemnation if I am in Christ! But I must never minimize or deny what I have done, if it is wrong.

I am free to confess my sin because of the power of the Blood that has cleansed me. I have grace from God to get up and press on in faith once I have dealt with my sin. Lingering in condemnation produces morbid shame that keeps me in a pit of despair and is spiritually unproductive. Shame as an emotion is helpful for remorse, that I may appreciate the gravity of my sin's effect on another. But when shame is not answered by repentance and truth, it becomes a way of life. It turns morbid, distorting the character of God as well as my own.

To give an example of the effects of morbid shame in my own life, let me share a picture the Spirit gave me about how I once saw the Lord and myself:

There was a very wealthy man who came down to the pier where a large ship was docked. He came and told everyone that the ship, the cargo, the company, and everything, now belonged to him. In acquiring everything he wanted, he also bought a rat that was living in the bottom of the cargo hold. The rat was me. I was purchased along with the boat, but I was not what he desired. I was now His, only because I was hidden among the other things the buyer really wanted. This is how I viewed my being bought by the Blood of Christ!

What's wrong with this picture? First of all, I had a **conceit** (a self-serving agenda) that in order to be loved by God, I had to be someone He desired for some value I had in myself. He would only love those who fulfilled some self-interest He had, or whose personality He enjoyed being around. God was just like everybody else.

Second, because I was a hopelessly corrupt person, I could not possibly find a way to be loved by God. So, I had another **conceit** that I might as well keep on sinning because I couldn't win God's affection anyway. I wrung my hands with self-pity and consoled myself with more sin. This kind of thinking followed me after my conversion, even though I knew better. I excused myself from difficult stands of faith because I continued in the self-serving **conceit** of believing I didn't matter.

The truth is that God is Love. He loves the worthless in spite of themselves: while we were still sinners, Jesus died for us all. God cannot deny His Own Nature, which is to love! I was not just allowed in on the deal because He loved everyone else. This is reverse grandiosity—that I'm exceptional in some negative way. I was also thinking I was capable of exhausting God's grace, until He said to me, "Do you think the suffering and Blood of My Son were NOT enough for YOU? Something MORE than the Blood is needed to make YOU acceptable?" I stood corrected.

Shame Sources

Shame becomes rooted in me through sinful acts that were done to me *by* others, as well as sinful acts I have done *to* others. These humiliating events and experiences are numerous in their expression. They are wounds that need healing. Some may even be traumatic. A partial list would include rape, incest, abortion, betrayal, beatings, maiming, being abandoned, leaving my marriage, rejection, divorce, cheating my marriage vow with one who is not my mate, cheating on my marriage vow by withholding sex from my mate, excessive control, bullying, promiscuity, pornography, prostitution, misogyny (hating woman), misandry (hating men), emasculation (social castration), racial bigotry, addiction, slander, anger storms, passive-aggressive behavior, theft, murder, degrading assessments, violation of intimacy, lies, withholding affection...

Most of the examples above are sins of activity. There are also many sins of passivity, or refusing to take righteous action. These kinds of sins are a refusal to confront evil, refusal to exhort, refusal to help, refusal to sacrifice, a refusal to speak up or testify, refusal to take responsibility, refusal to praise, refusal to confess, refusal to make amends, laziness, procrastination, wallowing in self-pity, staying comfy, hiding, pretending to have other more pressing matters, quenching faith by staying selfish, helpless, and afraid...

Wounds that we receive can make us victims, and alas, victims have great potential to become the victimizers of others, actively or passively. Shame is a reflexive response to hide what has happened, but through shame, we also deprive ourselves of help. We want to hide what we have done, just like Adam and Eve. Some of us block the significance of the painful truth with shutdowns, or minimize the true significance with rationalization, or justify it with excuses. Some of us resort to medicating ourselves with chemicals or compulsive behaviors. Some of us artfully redesign our memories to create something completely false. Some of us go on a rampage of self-entitled revenge, creating more to be ashamed of when we come to our senses.

But, it is a holy thing to confront my unholiness. To do this honestly, I must *know* I am under the Blood, I must *know* I am forgiven, and I must *know* who I am in Christ and I must *know* Christ is in me. The Shame Inventory should begin as a black and white self-analysis, raw and unbalanced, without justifications or excuses. Balance will return in the later steps of this process, but first, the sin must be fearlessly exposed for what it is. *This is about finding Satan's ways in me from my past, so I will not so easily be fooled again by his lies to my soul.* If I am born again, all these things have already been forgiven.

I found my own shame inventory to be very revealing. Through my wounds, I saw much more clearly the embedded shame that was corrupting my faith, my perceptions, and my behaviors:

- I saw how a man-who-hurts, hurts others and continues to hurt himself.

- Shame gave me an excuse to act out to comfort myself, to sell out to protect my selfishness, and to procrastinate in order to delay being responsible.

- My shame caused me to attach my self-worth to my personal circumstances, not to Jesus. Real cause and effect were confused and distorted. Small criticisms seemed like attacks on my value as a person, when they were sometimes given as helpful, candid advice. Shame was an automatic interpreter that made things mean something that was not necessarily true. My shame was unable to distinguish between what was an insult and what was not.

- My shame made chronic self-mockery and even self-curses a reflexive response to even the most trivial mistakes I made. My sudden flashes of anger were often out of proportion to what happened. My outraged *vanity* expected perfection. Shame triggered grandiosity as a false compensation—as if I am supposed to be Great!

- My shame gave me frequent irrational nightmares, unfounded insecurities, and profound self-hatred.

- It reinterpreted many of my weaknesses as occasions to despise myself in comparison to others; it made me jealous of them and ungrateful to God about how I was made.

What I was doing was ruining all my relationships. My *secretiveness* was withholding intimacy from others. My *anger flashes* frightened them away. My *ruthlessness* repelled them. My *gossip* betrayed them. My *treachery* appalled them. My *praise seeking* manipulated them. My *self-pity* disgusted them. My *controlling behavior* wore them out. My *insensitivity* devalued them. My *selfishness* ripped them off. My *envy* made them feel guilty about what they had. My *arguing* created division. My *slander* tore them down. My *melancholy* shut them out. My *conceit* bullied them. My *deceit* exploited them. My *grandiosity* created false hope. My *escapism* abandoned them. My *laziness* devalued them. My *lust* objectified them. My *lying* destroyed their trust. My *despair* drained them... These same things I did to provoke others I also did to God.

My motives were all about myself. I believed my own way was the way to get what I wanted. I also knew that some of the things I wanted were *not* what God or other people wanted for me to have or do. Good motives come from a righteous heart. Bad motives come from a sinful heart. Self-centered living was destroying everything that was good, and it was destroying me. How could I begin to undo all the damage I had caused? I needed to man-up to the truth, and learn to live in good faith with those around me.

My Shame Inventory

To break the power of shame, I must break the system of **lie set-ups, false payoffs,** and **conceits** that have been woven into my beliefs, attitudes, and behavior—as habits. I found the following inventory process to be very helpful and healing. There are seven columns in it. Follow the directions at the end of each chapter on what to consider for each.

THE SHAME INVENTORY

Column 1 MY SHAMEFUL MEMORIES 30-40 EXAMPLES	Col- umn 2 HOW WAS I HURT?	Column 3 HOW DID I HURT OTHERS?	Column 4 HOW DID I GET REVENGE OR CONSOLE MYSELF?	Column 5 WHAT DID I WRONGLY BELIEVE ABOUT ME?	Column 6 HOW WAS GOD'S TRUTH CORRUPTED?	Column 7 WHAT IS THE BIBLICAL TRUTH?
1						
2-40						

In **Chapter 1**, you will begin by listing shameful memories in Column 1 on your **Shame Inventory** sheet. Once you have 30–40 examples, you will have a large enough sample to expose patterns of thinking and behavior.

The greatest benefit comes from doing one column at a time, moving down through the whole list sequentially. Be patient with yourself and trust God for breakthroughs. You will experience some painful recall in the process, but joy and freedom will follow if you persevere in faith to the end. God means this process for healing, not condemnation nor does He wish to provoke a relapse. So shame the devil—confess your sin.

ASSIGNMENT
Column 1 on the Chart: SHAMEFUL MEMORIES.
List any shameful act that becomes a trigger for shame in you and provokes painful recall when it comes to mind. It can be either something that was done to you or something you did to others, or

something you did to disgrace yourself even if no one else appeared to be harmed. Do not stop until you have 30-40 examples.

Carrying a small note book around with you may be easier than trying to write them all in one sitting. Write the examples shame *incidents*, or *events*, or *situations* as they come to mind, then go about your daily business. If you are having difficulty getting **30 – 40** examples, you may be blocking. Ask the Lord to help you remember more. It may also be that your examples are too general, like: I treat women badly, or I try to control men. There may be 8 - 10 specific examples packed inside either of those categories. Be specific, list each one. Or you might use a mood or an emotion as a trigger. Don't do that. Write a specific *incident memory* that provoked the mood. You will easily fill your list if you are honest and patient with yourself.

2

Sharper Than A Two-edged Sword

Lord, please help me to begin to understand how You have made me and how the enemy has been able to misuse me.

Hebrews 4:12 says:

> For the Word of God is living and active, sharper than any two-edged sword, piercing to the division of soul and of spirit, of joints and of marrow, and discerning the thoughts and intentions of the heart. – ESV

The Word is able to pierce the thoughts and intentions of my heart, to distinguish between my perceptions and motives, exposing agendas and self-serving **conceits** that give me permission to sin. The emotion I experience in my soul can also be misinterpreted as discernment in my spirit if I do not understand the self-interest focus of my soul versus the God-interest focus of my spirit (see diagram on **page 40**). My soul has its affections and desires, and my spirit also has its affections and desires. How am I to know what is going on inside me if I am unaware of the **creational focus**, or functional agendas of these two distinct parts of me? Because both are invisible, the Two-edged Sword of the Word of God is necessary to tell them apart. We shall continue to wield the sword of the Word to that end.

36

David speaks to his own soul repeatedly in the Psalms. Of note are **Psalm 42:5,11** and **Psalm 43:5**, where he says three times:

> Why are you cast down O my *soul*, and why are *you* in turmoil within me? – ESV

What the spirit and the soul share is invisibility. We all know we can't slice open the brain and find mind or emotions. We cannot see where the spirit or soul of a person is that way either. But they apparently do have subtle boundaries only the sharpness of the sword of the Word of God can separate. By knowing the piercing Word (**logos**), we can know what is of God and what is not, as well as what is spirit and what is soul.

The New Testament refers to believers as the temple of God. **1 Corinthians 3:16** says:

> Do you not know that you are God's temple [**naos**] and that God's Spirit dwells in you? – ESV [Shank]

An individual believer is also a temple. **I Corinthians 6:15-20** says:

> Do you not know that your bodies are members of Christ himself? Shall I then take the members of Christ and unite them with a prostitute? Never! Do you not know that he who unites himself with a prostitute is one with her in body? For it is said, "The two will become one flesh." But whoever is united with the Lord is one with him in spirit.

> Flee from sexual immorality. All other sins a person commits are outside the body, but whoever sins sexually, sins against their own body. Do you not know that your bodies are temples [**naos**] of the Holy Spirit, who is in you, whom you have received from God? You are not your own; you

were bought at a price. Therefore honor God with your bodies. – NIV [Shank]

The temple in Israel described in the Old Testament had three distinct parts:

1. The Outer Court had a physical presence all could see. This is like my body, which gives me a presence in the physical world, and enables me to know and experience that world in all my days under the sun.

2. Inside the court was the Holy Place, which was closed off to the outside world—it was lit by the inner lampstand. This is much like the light of my own mind in introspection concerning my feelings, thoughts, and reflexive opinions. This is what my soul does, making it possible for me to know myself, care for myself, and be able to relate to the experiences of other souls around me.

3. Behind that chamber was the Holy of Holies (the **naos**), where the Mercy Seat was placed, separated only by a curtain from the Holy Place. This room was only illuminated inside by the presence of the Lord Himself—corresponding to my human spirit as the container of the Holy Spirit—making it possible for me to intimately know God and His ways, as well as know myself in relation to Him. It also means that His Spirit indwelling me causes me to never be separated from God, even though my soul feelings may say He is not there.

Before the indwelling of the Holy Spirit, which made me a child of God in Jesus Christ, my spirit contained the spirit of this world—

Satan, *the Author of Sin*. At conversion, Satan's slave-to-sin old nature was evicted, and my spirit was cleansed and restored to the purpose for which it was created, to be the dwelling place of God—*the Author of Righteousness*. I am now a slave to righteousness but may not be aware of this at all experientially if I have *not yet believed* I am a new creation in Christ—and that my old nature is now dead. This reality can only be experienced by putting this biblical truth about me into practice with choices that *act as if* the Word of God is true, whether it looks or feels like it is true, to my soul.

I AM A TEMPLE OF GOD

BODY
creational focus:
I experience the physical world through my senses to satisfy my bodily *needs, appetites* and *desires*. Satan tries to get me to misuse the weaknesses of my body's needs, appetites, and desires, to cause me to sin.

SOUL
creational focus:
My soul is concerned with my *value, purpose* and *self-interests*. It uses my mind, emotions and imagination to assess what is happening. Satan tries to turn my self-interest focus into selfishness.

SPIRIT
creational focus:
My human spirit gives me the capacity to commune with God. By my spirit's union with Him I am able to know Him intimately. *He who has the Spirit of Christ is one spirit with Him.* When I did not have His Spirit in me, spiritual things made no sense because my human spirit was evil. Satan tries to block communion with God, even if I have the Spirit of Christ in me.

God designed my **body (soma)** to care for itself, to be concerned about my need for physical well-being, safety, and satisfaction. This is a good thing. But Satan corrupts my natural need for rest into laziness; he corrupts my need for food into overeating and drunkenness; he corrupts my drive to reproduce into fornication or pornography. He also misuses the strength of my body—to do work or to protect the weak—into a tool for violence. Every God-designed need and drive is twisted by the devil's evil influence, to take advantage of me. Sin trained my body to expect to get its way and to control my choices through my fleshly weakness, in order to do harm.

But if I become a Christian, I must remember that my spirit has changed but my flesh, the natural part of me, will *always oppose* my spirit. It will still feel pulls to pride, lust, envy, et cetera. My flesh hates obedience, patience, and self-control. But I am now the master of my flesh and can learn to overcome. In Christ, my flesh is mine, but it is not me.

My **soul (psyche)** is focused on my value, my purpose, and my self-interest; and it is designed to see what is in my interest, to feel the meaning and gravity of it in my emotions, and to use the imagination of my mind to interpret opportunities or threats in relation to me and mine. But it is important to remember that my soul is only giving me an *opinion* based on limited knowledge. Satan wants to corrupt all these God-given abilities, to get the self-interest focus of my soul to act out in selfishness, causing my focus to be *exclusively* on ME. He wants to bend me away from God's will, so I will do the evil the devil wants me to do.

The devil does not want me to see or feel the effect of my sin on others. He wants me to misremember what happened with a good excuse, so I can continue to have a high reason to do a low thing. He deceives me into believing my faith is subject to my *mood*, so my faithfulness goes up and down by how I feel at the moment. Through this kind of manipulation, I will stay immature and unfruitful—not to mention unfaithful. I will not be able to build anything of real value because I will start something when I feel in-spired but leave it unfinished when I feel discouraged.

Satan wants me to believe that what I *feel or imagine* to be the truth about my situation or options is the whole story. He wants me to make my choices by how things may appear—according to what he tries to convince me is in the self-interest of my soul. He does not want me to believe that what the Word of God says is true. Evil does not want me to learn to walk by the Spirit.

If my **spirit (pneuma)** is not joined to the Holy Spirit, I will not be able to break out of my sin patterns. But if I receive Christ, God puts His Holy Spirit in me and I can begin to use His power, wisdom, and love to learn how to become a whole new person. He will give me the grace to learn His new ways. His Holy Spirit in me makes me a new creation in Christ—a Christ person! I can now stand be-fore God without shame because of His forgiveness. I can forgive those who have hurt me and my wounds can begin to heal. I can show His love to those I have hurt in the past by making a sincere amends, so they too, may begin to heal. In Christ, I can now deal with my consequences, the difficulty of my circumstances, or the hopeless feelings in my **soul**. Christ in me will overcome through me. But I must learn to believe and obey Him. My human spirit must be empowered by the Holy Spirit.

Many of us consider ourselves to be Christians because we are in mental agreement with the historical fact that Jesus died for our sins. But as Jesus said to Nicodemus, unless a person is born again, he cannot enter the Kingdom of Heaven. This means I must make a spiritual transaction with God—where I give myself to Him and He gives Himself to me. It is also about being willing to follow Him in the obedience of faith. If you have doubts about your standing in

Christ, I invite you to consider the points in the following prayer, which is quite thorough:

House Cleaning Prayer

Father God in heaven, I believe Jesus is Your only begotten Son, Who was born in the flesh like me, was tempted in every way as I am, but without sinning, and that He suffered and died in my place to pay for all my sin. Then He rose from the dead and is now seated at Your Right Hand, in heaven.

I freely confess to being a sinner who desperately needs the Blood of Jesus to be saved. I agree with You, Lord, that I am guilty of all the sins Your Holy Spirit has shown me to be wrong.

I renounce Satan and all his works in my life, and I turn away from him to serve my new Master, the Lord Jesus Christ.

I renounce the lies from Satan that I have believed, as the Holy Spirit reveals those lies to me.

I renounce my bitterness and rights to revenge, which I have held against You, Lord, and those who have harmed me.

I renounce my fears that Satan has used to cause me to block my conscience, steal my boldness, and withhold love from You, Lord, and those around me.

I renounce my shame that Satan has used to make me a liar, a deceiver, and one who tries to hide from Your Goodness, O Lord.

Father, I do not deserve Your mercy, but please be merciful to me and forgive me for all my sins, because of what Your Righteous Son has done in love for me. Teach me what You are really like by show-ing me Your Truth and Your Lovingkindness.

Please fill me with Your Holy Spirit that I may be born again as a new creation in Christ, with *the power to repent and follow* You faithfully, and to bear Your fruit of righteousness in my life.

Open Your Word to me that I may learn Your living wisdom.

Heal my bitterness as I learn to forgive those who harm me, that I may become sweet.

May Your Word fill me with faith to face all my fears with righteous courage and help me to be quick to confess and repent when I have sinned.

Please clothe the nakedness of my shame. And please deliver me from habits of willful disobedience.

Receive me now into Your keeping and lead me to a strong Bible believing church where I may be baptized and become a disciple.

I thank You Lord and trust that You will give me the grace I need for my weaknesses, so I may be able to follow You faithfully, in Je-sus' Wonderful Name, amen!

If you have just prayed this prayer, receive these words of bless-ing because they are for you:

May the Lord anoint you with His Holy Spirit because you have be-lieved in your heart, and have confessed with your lips that Jesus is Lord. May His Spirit fill you and lift your spirit with the power to overcome evil. May the eyes of your heart be opened to His Wonders and His Lovingkindness. May He open His Word to you with wisdom and understanding. And may the Lord refresh you, heal you, and keep you in Jesus' Wonderful Name, amen!

After having prayed a prayer like the one above, you are ready to learn how to walk in the spirit. Your conscience must be guided by the Holy Spirit through your human **spirit** where you can know and experience God, Who is Spirit. He will speak to you. He will hear you. He will show you. You will see what He wants you to see. Without the guidance of the Holy Spirit in you, your human conscience will default to the selfishness of Satan, to misuse your **soul** to harm the bodies and souls of others.

A Definition of the Soul (from Deep Discipling / Shank)

I see the soul in this way: My soul makes it possible for my spirit to be personally engaged with the world around my body. But it tends to be *subjective* in its response—that is: how does this look from my self-interest point-of-view or agenda. Yet, my soul enables the meaning and gravity of my circumstances to be experienced. So, I hear someone insult me and it wounds me emotionally—another expresses appreciation and I feel elated. I read of dire prospects in the economy in the newspaper, and my mind perceives the gravity of the impending possibilities.

However, it's very important to understand that my soul is gauging information based on its impact on me or on others who matter to me—*what would it be like if what happened to you happened to me?* This is a good thing to be able to do, because empathy with others is not possible without being able to identify myself with the experiences of others. And if I cannot perceive and experience my own life because of emotional blocking, I can't relate to God or others in any meaningful way, either.

If the soul is the result of the union of Adam's clay body and the living breath of God, I believe the soul has an intended function to *link* my body to my spirit. I am one person, not two or three. There is an intended continuity in God's design of me. My soul perceives bodily sensation and translates it into a meaningful experience. It has been helpful to learn to see these perceptions as *opinions* and not necessarily facts about what is happening, or what I need to do about it. My soul is about my self-interest—what is good for me. Are my needs being met? Am I safe? Am I respected? Am I fulfilled? Is there any danger of losing anything or anyone who matters to me? I believe Satan works through the weakness of my flesh to bend me toward his ends, by corrupting my soul's self-interested focus, into selfishness. In this way, Satan misuses God's intended design in order to distract me from the will of the Lord.

But my soul needs to take direction from the Spirit of God, if indeed I have the Spirit of God in my human **spirit**. Sometimes God may want me to go against what is in my self-interest or to do things my soul would not prefer to do, for the sake of the kingdom and His goodness toward others. I am finite; only God is infinite. I am limited in my perception, but God is eternal and sees all. My mind knows little, but His Mind is universal and knows all, even the end from the beginning.

Imagine a giant ballroom with a plush carpet. God is universal. His mind is as big as the ballroom. In comparison, my mind is a small speck of dust, lost in the strands of the carpet. The little self-interest voice of my **soul** may say: *Why is God doing that? Why isn't God doing anything about my problem?* I am completely ignorant of the vast complexity of things God is working together for His good purposes. My speck of understanding cannot begin to comprehend it all; that's why He expects me to have faith in Him for all that is going on around me. Thank God, He didn't make knowledge and understanding the standard of acceptance! The ballroom will never fit inside my speck, but my speck is in Christ at the Right Hand of God. I need only to do what He shows me.

By being reborn in Christ, my human **spirit** is now able to borrow from the Mind of God what I need for the moment I am in. I will never be able to comprehend more than a fraction of what God is doing in the economy of His purposes. I will never know all, but I can trust in the One Who does know all, the One Who loves me. He knows all the hidden factors, circumstances, and agendas of heaven and earth, and *He has already taken into consideration my incompetence in His plan for my life.* So, God only asks me to *trust* Him and obey what He directs me to do—to live by faith. All that really matters now is that I do the next thing in faith and leave everything that follows for the Lord to manage. In this way, His yoke is light.

Satan didn't want to do that. He wanted to go his own way. And he makes it a point of pride to resist the will of God by urging me to go my own way as well. But if I listen to him, I'm only going his way, not my way. I was made in the image of God, made to be like Jesus and to do the will of the Lord.

Therefore, my **soul** not only has the capacity to experience what is happening around me, but it is also aware of the creational needs and appetites of my body. When my **spirit** was joined to the spirit of the world, Satan was able to take advantage of my weaknesses to gratify the needs of my body *without regard* for its intended use, *without regard* for the hopes and desires of others, and *without regard* for what God wanted. So, the procreative desire intended for marriage becomes fornication. The desire for justice becomes revenge and unforgiveness. Satan appeals to the self-interest focus of my soul to entice me to self-gratification at the expense of others. Even when I am a Christian, he tries to get me to believe I can act on behalf of myself *without regard* for what my True Lord wants. Every time I disobey God as a Christian, I obey a **lie**. The more lies I believe, the harder my heart becomes. The harder my heart becomes the more evil fruit I will produce, discrediting my testimony and disgracing the True Lord Who is in me. The eyes of my heart then become blind, and my mind is darkened, until I repent.

There was a time in my life when I nearly gave up on trying to overcome, because disobedience reduced me to believing "I'm just a sinner saved by grace." But this self-serving **conceit** gave me an excuse to sin. The more I gave in to the strong pulls of temptation through my flesh, the more my conscience was bent to believing my flesh was *who I really was*. Therefore, I became hopeless and the victory that was supposed to be mine in Christ was impossible. Believing this lie made God's Word seem like a lie! So the ultimate in repentance is to believe I am not what my flesh says I am.

The Soul & the Addiction Cycle

In addition to the bad code the enemy has used to misdirect my mind, he also finds opportunity in the cycles of my emotions and moods to provoke compulsive behavior. This compulsive behavior is the real addiction—the process addiction that drives all other addictive behaviors.

Start at the top and proceed clockwise.

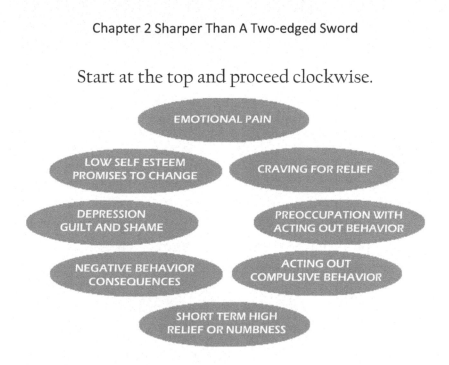

1. The cycle begins at the top of the chart with EMOTIONAL PAIN. There is real pain here from my wounds, anger over offenses, fears about what could happen again, and shame about my behavior in response to the pain of my wounds.

2. Moving clockwise, emotional pain leads to a CRAVING FOR RELIEF. Who doesn't want the pain to stop? The question is, will I turn to God or Notgod, Christ or Satan? Do I want to fix my problems, or do I just want to fix my pain?

3. The desire for relief becomes PREOCCUPATION WITH ACTING OUT BEHAVIOR, which grows stronger and stronger as a temptation. Because of longstanding habits learned from my old master, my flesh is eager for the old solution, even though I now have a new nature in Christ. I must learn new habits of believing and response.

4. I make a choice to ACT OUT COMPULSIVE BEHAVIOR, choosing to believe I cannot suffer withdrawal with endurance, so I succumb to acting out in the old ways.

5. Acting out creates a SHORT-TERM HIGH, RELIEF OR NUMBNESS. The pain is momentarily relieved with pleasure or satisfaction, revenge or comfort. But I have only temporarily jumped into unreality without solving any of my problems. My conscience has now been dulled. My focus is distracted. I am emotionally insensitive. I have become unaware of the matters at hand which need my attention.

6. The temporary numbness is followed by NEGATIVE BEHAVIOR CONSEQUENCES. My insensitivity causes blunders in judgment, alienation of friends and family, poor job performance, and it is a huge waste of time.

7. These consequences produce DEPRESSION, GUILT AND SHAME. When reality inevitably returns, I am painfully aware of *some* of what I have done. I have no excuses for the damage I have caused, though I try to justify myself. I blame God for how He made me, or I blame you. I insult you by minimizing my offenses with excuses. I insult God by minimizing my confession. Or, ashamed of myself, I try to hide from both.

8. The depression, guilt, and shame lead me once again to LOW SELF ESTEEM, SELF LOATHING and PROMISES TO CHANGE. Because my guilt and shame are stabbing me with the sharp point of consequences, I feel remorse. But my remorse is more about myself—my flesh, so I hate myself. I

feel hopeless, but I hate feeling hopeless, so my remorse becomes shallow and does not last. I promise to change. But I cannot fully change my ways without changing my operator (**energeo**). If my operator is now Christ, I must learn how to draw on His power in me to be transformed into His likeness, to be able to suffer change. My flesh is hopeless, it cannot be reformed. *I must start seeing that what my flesh wants is not what the real me in Christ wants!* Then, the sooner I intercept the cycle with the truth, the easier it is to break out of this loop.

Healing and Brain Training

It has been interesting for me to learn that most brain activity in the course of a day is carried out by the unconscious mind. Situation number 1 has a learned A B C response. Situation 2 has an X Y Z learned response, et cetera.

On the other hand, the learning process takes conscious effort by my mind, with focused power and sometimes draining fatigue. But, repetition allows my mind to learn a new skill or behavior as a new habit. Then, my brain delegates the new learned behavior to my unconscious mind, which makes an automatic response possible—conserving brain energy. The deceiver wants to infect my natural habit formation process so evil agendas and responses are normalized and go largely undetected by my conscious mind. He wants me to react to triggers without thinking about where they might take me. Evil wants to set a precedent in my behavior that is corrupted by lies, that my brain will then normalize through repetition.

By the time compulsive behavior becomes a full-blown addiction, acting out has caused my brain to normalize the intensified levels of its own chemical stimulation or sedation. This causes an altered adjustment of my brain's chemical *normalcy bias*—what my brain has learned to experience as normal. Since I am not a scientist, I can't specifically explain how behavior affects brain chemistry or how, in turn, brain chemistry affects behavior. But understanding what the power of my *choices* will produce in response to what *voice* I obey, is of the utmost importance. Who is the master of my choice, Christ or Satan?

As I have just said, similar events trigger similar responses. Repetition of habits allow my brain to respond to the same triggers without having to rethink the process again. I know the addicted brain's normalcy bias does not think things are normal unless it has regular large charges of the stimulating brain chemicals that are created by intense mood alteration activity. I also know destructive habits were learned by my body and my soul from my old operator. This is my flesh contending with my spirit, demanding satisfaction.

My new operator is Jesus Christ, and I am a new creation in Him. His Holy Spirit is teaching me new habits of believing that are exposing and destroying my former **conceits**, while strengthening my perseverance in faith. I have learned that withdrawal from the old habits is survivable. Giving in to sin does not have to be inevitable. My brain is learning a new normal. My healing began with His Blood, which justifies me, and with receiving His Holy Spirit, Who empowers and sanctifies me. My healing is increased by learning what this all means. By acting *as if* what the Word says is true in my choices, I'm learning more and more how to bear His fruit because He is making me a willing slave of righteousness.

ASSIGNMENT

Column 2 on the Shame Inventory Chart: HOW WAS I HURT? The information below is offered to help you see actions and motives that may apply in your process. Use whatever may apply as you write your responses to each shame event in **Column 2** on your chart sheets.

FOR EXAMPLE: Was my value and dignity stripped from me? Was I abandoned, engulfed by control, or abused? What loss did I suffer? In what ways did I lose my sense of confidence, or made to feel inferior? In what ways did I lose the capacity to trust? How did I lose the respect or my reputation with people who know me? How was I seduced or betrayed...?

Apply these kinds of conclusions to each of your examples wherever they fit in **Column 2**.

Column 3 on the Shame Inventory Chart: HOW DID I HURT OTHERS? The information below is offered to help you see actions and motives that may apply in your process. Use whatever may apply as you write your responses to each shame event in **Column 3** on your chart sheets.

FOR EXAMPLE: How was value and dignity stripped from the one I harmed? Was he or she abandoned, engulfed by control, or abused? What loss did the one I harmed suffer? In what ways did the one I hurt lose self-confidence, or be made to feel inferior? In what ways did the one I hurt lose the capacity to trust? How did what I have done cause others to lose respect or reputation with those around them? How were they seduced and betrayed by me? In what ways were they provoked to sin because of what I did...?

Summarize how others were hurt by you in **Column 3**.

Some examples from your shame list will be about your wounds from others in **Column 2**. Some of your examples will be about your wounding of others in **Column 3**. Some wounds will affect both **Columns 2 & 3**.

3

True And False Affections

O Lord, purify my desires that I may know and learn to express real love.

I have found that many people do not really want deep intimacy though they say they do. They want to be loved, but they do not want to pay the price of love. People don't want to be lonely, but they don't want to go out of their way to really care about someone else. My flesh only wants to be cared for, but the Spirit of Christ in me is willing to make real love sacrifices in caring for another. It is in the self-interest of my soul to love and be loved. Selfishness of my flesh wants to be loved and understood, but easily tires of doing the same in return.

Rabbi Dr. Abraham Twerski on his *Fish Love* YouTube video says: "You say you love fish? Then why do you take it out of the water to kill it and eat it? You do not love fish, you love yourself." So much of what we say and do in the name of love is only fish love.

"A man says he loves a woman because she is supposed to fulfill all his physical needs. She says she loves a man who is supposed to meet all her emotional needs. But each is looking out for his/her own needs. Fish love is primarily about personal gratification. This is not love for the other to meet the other's needs, it's about what I am going to get, not about what I am going to give."

This is a self-for-self deal—not the self-for-another **agape** love in Scripture, which comes from the nature of God. Dr. Twerski goes on to say that a serious mistake we make is that we think we give to those we love, (to get something in return) but the truth is, *we love those to whom we give* (even if we receive nothing in return).

When I wrote about the soul in **Chapter 2**, I said the soul has a creational focus on what is in my self-intertest. Self-love is what the soul does in looking out for itself. *Jesus does not condemn that*, but says we are to love others *as* we love ourselves. Without self-love I cannot perceive the gravity of my choices and consequences. My soul's self-love knows what hurts me and also what blesses me. The Lord's intent is that I use my own experience to be able to create empathy with you, through what I perceive to be your experience—especially so I will realize the effects of what I do to you that either hurts or blesses. Then I will do unto you what I want done unto me, and I will not do unto you what I do not want done unto me.

Deals and plays

My flesh wants to make deals or make plays for what it wants. When my soul follows the desires of my flesh, my actions become selfish—fish love. It is a deal I make with another fish lover. What do I mean when I say I love you? What was my motive in offering that deal? What was my payoff in taking this deal? Why did I make that play? How did I use you? How did you use me? What made me think *that* was good or right?

56

she was a rose
and they picked her.
not for a life with her.
just to watch her wither.
—from *SECRET SERMONS* by **Victoria Hope Peterson**

Who really wants to be a "baby momma" or a perpetual "fiancé" with three kids, but not be a treasured and protected wife? Why would a woman be a mistress and betray another woman by stealing the heart of another's husband, and seriously wounding their children—as well as her own? What kind of a man mistreats a woman like this in the name of love? What kind of a man would steal the heart of another man's wife, to seriously wound that man and his children—or his own? Fish-love does not consider putting a woman in a situation of having to choose between poverty and hardship as a single parent, or killing that child with an abortion— to escape that poverty fate. Fish love does not consider the rights of the preborn child, either. There is more hope for the shameful than for the shameless.

"When women without virtue give themselves to men without honor, they kill their own children or bring them up without fathers." — from *Away From You* / Shank / Peniel Music

It is wonderful news to realize all these sins can be forgiven through the Blood of Jesus—even if I have blood on my own hands. But the Lordship of Jesus must be confessed. And my sins must also be confessed, not justified with excuses. What I have advocated which is wrong must be renounced and turned away from, or my shame will not go away.

Fish love that is not satisfied can easily become misogyny (hating

57

women) or emasculation (humiliating men). A fish-loving man thinks he can wash the woman off of himself he has just used to meet his physical need. But he can't. A fish-loving woman will use a man to see if she can catch him for herself to meet her emotional needs, because "If I don't sleep with him, Sally will get him—then who will care for me?"

I believe a world-wide sexual plague is coming in these last days, like what happened in Central Africa where a whole generation of children had to be raised by their grandparents because their natural parents were dead and dying from AIDS. Our friends-with-benefits culture is a breeding ground for plagues like this. The number of sexually transmitted diseases that no longer respond to treatment are increasing. Virginity is mocked, covenants are easily abandoned for selfish reasons. Fish love abounds! In my youth, I committed some of these same sins. Now I deeply regret them and have made amends to many of those whom I have harmed.

As we judge others, so are we to be judged, unless we repent and change our ways. Because they did not repent, the slaughtering place for the people of Jerusalem when the Babylonians conquered them was the **Valley of Tophet. (Jeremiah 7:30-34)** This was the very place where their innocent children were buried, who were sacrificed to the pagan gods, so their parents would have a better life. Are men and women not meant to bless each other and protect their innocent children? God's intention was to show how no one can bless a man like a loving wife. And no woman can be blessed more than by a loving husband. A man and a woman should bless their child, not sacrifice it to pay for their own sin.

Micah 6:7b says:
> Shall I give my firstborn for my transgression,
> the fruit of my body for the sin of my soul? – ESV

Infatuation

New love often begins with the magnetic attraction of infatuation. Each sees the other as perfect and everything the other does is wonderful. But this is not real love yet. It is just a fish-love deal—*I am getting a perfect lover!* But the root word in infatuation is from fatuous, which means foolish. So, to be in a state of infatuation could be said to be in a state of "enfoolishment." It is exciting and fun to be attracted to each other in this way, but it is a great mistake to move quickly into consummation (sexual union) while infatuation is driving the relationship. Real self-for-others love for someone cannot happen until there is a mutual exchange of faults.

Sexual consummation is rightly reserved by God for marriage. When I have faith and the courage to risk losing you, whom I say I love, by sharing the truth about myself, I am truly loving and protecting your life and heart. My past and my present circumstances are important for you to know. Just as infatuation strongly attracts, sexual union binds us together. But if that binding together happens without a season of truth in abstinence, (courtship) each may feel manipulated or even betrayed by the other once the truth eventually comes out. I must put my fishlove to death in Christ with the truth. Sometimes this will cause a breakup because the truth about one of us is more than the other can live with.

But it is better to find that out before a covenant is made and dependent children add more stress to a relationship built on fishlove. Children are seriously harmed when they see their parents hating each other. Once the truth has been told and each sees the other's flaws, then real **agape**—godly self-for-others love—is possible, because we are making an informed choice to commit to each other knowing the facts and trusting God in self-control.

When my wife and I were courting, we agreed to abstain from sex until we were married. During that time we talked about our past. We shared our baggage and consequences. My history had more consequences than hers and some of them were hard for her to hear. She needed time to get over her disappointment in me from my past. She needed to be confident that I was no longer the same person I was before she could make a covenant with me. I needed to give her whatever time she needed to decide what her heart wanted to do. I named my problems but I did not dump all the details. I let her decide how far she wanted to go with the information. I surrendered to whatever God wanted to do through her. When she was reassured that I was no longer the man I had been, she finally agreed to marry me.

The Power of Procreation

We were created in the image of God and commanded to keep and guard the earth in His Name. We were also given the power to multiply life in producing children. The way we use this power to bring life into the world matters. If what we do does not matter, we don't matter and the people we say we love don't matter. But because our choices matter, we matter. We are answerable for how we use this power which is entrusted to us by God.

Fish love of our children is wicked. If I cannot say "no" to myself, I cannot say "no" to my children. In an extreme example, I remember counseling a man in his recovery from meth addiction. As I visited him one day in rehab, I asked him how his daughters were doing. He said, "Oh, they're typical junkies, sleeping with their dealers to get free dope." I said to him, "why aren't you screaming and running down the street pulling out handfuls of your own hair in desperation over them?" Thoughtfully, he rested his chin in the palm of his hand as he leaned on the table, "Hmmm, why is that?"

Thankfully, this man has done a lot of hard self-examination since then and God has helped him to stay sober and be successful with his job. He is now actively pursuing his daughters and at this writing, they are sober and going to church with him. His past drug use had completely closed off his conscience. He was numb. And so were his daughters. His flesh did not want to do an inventory like this. Neither did my flesh back in the day. But as I have already said: It is a holy thing to confront my own unholiness.

Sexual Shame

Most of us find that our sexual histories have some of the deepest shaming wounds. Some were self-inflicted. Some shame comes from the way we wounded others. And some shame from wounds forced upon us.

For those of us who have been sexually abused, I strongly recommend *HEALING THE WOUNDED HEART,* by **Dan B. Allender**. In his book, the author describes the sexual predator's process of "grooming" the innocent or naïve by "reading" their prey and appealing to unmet needs, making him or her feel special. A false bond of trust is established, which is then exploited with arousal. Then the child or adolescent suffers betrayal and harm through sexual conquest. The victim is often left with *rage* over the violation, and with *shame* and guilt in the pleasure of the arousal, causing serious emotional conflict with lasting consequences. The trauma is hidden by secrets and buried deep inside.

Adult victims of sexual abuse are frequently plagued with an inability to emotionally and physically give themselves to their mates in response to what may well be genuinely caring and loving intentions by their marriage partner. Because genuine loving words and touch resemble the grooming tactics of the predator, those actions become triggers that cause the victim to emotionally relive the trauma of sexual abuse, provoking resistance and shutdowns that reject real and genuine intimacy. Similarly, the same exploitation of needs and vulnerabilities are also the strategies for seduction by a predator in dating situations as well—when their target mistakes the grooming process for love.

The ways we were parented and the ways we have parented our children are other deep sources of shame. Some of us are even afraid to become parents. Whatever has happened to us and whatever we have done to bring shame on ourselves has produced many sinful responses. Let us go forward in bringing more light, to expose the bad code evil has made into a lie set-up in our behavior.

The Strong Shame the Weak

The majority rules in a democracy. Otherwise a king, or a dictator, or a select group will rule. But justice must make equal provision for the rights of all. To rule is not necessarily to suppress, but it often happens—in governments as well as in families. Shame is a big part of it. A man can physically force his will over a woman. A woman can emotionally force her will over a man. Both can be desperate, both can be ruthless. Men and women shame each other with blame. Their children are also shamed.

In some families, the fathers abuse the mothers by force or with excessive control, teaching their sons to later do the same with their wives. Their daughters grow up to marry abusive men because it was normal for them to live like this. In other families, women emasculate their men with contempt, teaching their daughters to do likewise with their husbands, but their sons grow up to have contempt for women, with a deep-rooted misogyny. Their daughters are eventually abandoned when their husbands find respect elsewhere.

Racial groups shame and justify prejudice against each other through generalized blame. Political groups blame and shame their opponents. Through the lens of my shame, my wounded soul will be tempted to project blame on *all who are like the ones who hurt me.*

Some say that patriarchal systems and families are evil, let's make them matriarchal. But this is a cynical tactic that politicizes sin. Matriarchal families and systems are abusive too. The real problem is that the strong oppress the weak, those with advantage take advantage, and those with power want more. Sin is sin, no matter who does it. But God calls everyone to loving submission—even Christ.

1 Corinthians 11:3 says:
> But I want you to understand that the head of every man is Christ, the head of a wife is her husband, and the head of Christ is God.

Socrates said: "An unexamined life is not worth living." An honest examination of myself through the eyes of others can be very revealing. So what am I really like under pressure? What am I really like when I have power? What am I like when I am desperate? What am I like when I have secrets I can use against others? What am I like when I am powerless? What am I like when I think no one is looking? God has condemned us to chew on the fruit of the Tree of the

Knowledge of Good and Evil, all our days under the sun. "**You wanted it, now you've got it. I warned you!**" To hide from this duty is to become a fool.

ASSIGNMENT

Column 4 on the Shame Inventory Chart: HOW DID I GET REVENGE OR CONSOLE MYSELF? Now you are going to start to learn where and how evil has planted bad code in your habitual response to triggers. The information below is offered to help you see actions and motives that may apply in your process. Use whatever may apply as you write your responses to each shame event in **Column 4** on your sheets.

So ask yourself, in what ways did your sinful response change you from being a wounded victim into someone who wounds and makes victims of others?

FOR EXAMPLE: Did I steal something from you? Did I kill your reputation with slander? Did I tell lies to deceive you? Did I withhold love, respect, or affection? Was I violent? Did I try to control you? Did I destroy something you loved? Did I cut you off from my life? Was I passive-aggressive to get even? Did I manipulate or use you? Did I cheat you? Did I falsely accuse or exaggerate your wrongs? Did I abandon you? Was I disobedient? Did I break promises or contracts? Did I harbor misogyny against women? Did I emasculate men? Did I turn the tables on you when you were right about me? Did I make you bend your conscience to make you go my way? Did I provoke envy or jealousy in you to make you feel less?

Did I flaunt my beauty to control you? Was I sneering and catty? Did I force what I wanted to be true on you without regard for the truth? Did I just ditch you?

How did I comfort myself?
FOR EXAMPLE: Did I medicate with drugs or alcohol? Did I binge on sex or eat too much? Did I get satisfaction out of manipulation or using people? Did I put the blame on everybody else? Did I wallow in self-absorption? Did I look for free rides through being helpless? Was I impulsive in my spending and behavior? Did I baby myself with self-indulgence? Did I make myself superior by holding judgmental contempt? Did I preoccupy myself with my looks? Did I hide to avoid conflict? Did I shut down emotionally? Did I sabotage something good just because I could? Did I withhold love or help or support? Do I need to be in dominant control to protect myself? Do I need to be helpless to avoid hard choices? Am I defiant to resist authority and accountability? Am I compliant to stay under the radar? Did I play the victim to control others with shame or obligation?

Apply your honest responses to each example in **Column 4**.

4

Wrong Believing

Lord, help me to be tender in my heart, to unblock my conscience, and strengthen my will to obey You.

Faith, Heart, Will and Conscience

My will is my chooser, and I am free to choose because God is free to choose and I am in His image. He made me for eternal relationship with Him in righteousness. I do not live like an animal, which follows the narrow parameters of instinct in what it does—like ducks that fly south for the winter. My chooser is commanded by God to follow the mind of my regenerated spirit, not the mind of the flesh. I have found it helpful to see mind in this case as the *mindset* of the spirit or the *mindset* of the flesh. A mindset is a perspective that has the components of desire, motive, and agenda.

Galatians 5:16-17 says:

> But I say, walk by the Spirit, and you will not gratify the desires of the flesh. For the desires of the flesh are against the

66

Spirit, and the desires of the Spirit are against the flesh, for these are opposed to each other, to keep you from doing the things you want to do. - ESV

This is only true when my human spirit is joined to the Spirit of God. When my spirit was not joined to God, it cooperated with the flesh, as my old nature. The desire of my soul is focused on my self-interest, but my soul has only a subjective perception of what that actually is. Subjective truth is what I believe to be true by how things seem—like an opinion. Objective truth is a fact, whether I believe it is true or not—how a thing really is. (*See* **A definition of the soul** on page **45**)

Romans 10:8-11 says:

But what does it say? "The Word is near you, in your mouth and in your heart" (that is, the word of faith that we proclaim); because, if you confess with your mouth that Jesus is Lord and believe in your heart that God raised Him from the dead, you will be saved. For with the *heart* one believes and is justified, and with the *mouth* one confesses and is saved. For the Scripture says, "Everyone who believes will not be put to shame." - ESV

The Greek word for heart in this passage is **kardia**, from which the English gets the word *cardiac* referring to things relating to the physical heart. The New Testament also uses **kardia** when referring to the physical heart, but many other verses use **kardia** to mean something more than the blood pump in our bodies. Jesus says: "...out of the abundance of the heart his mouth speaks" (**Luke 6:45**) In those cases, the heart is playing a vital role in expressing or suppressing right believing. My understanding of this is shown in the following diagram:

67

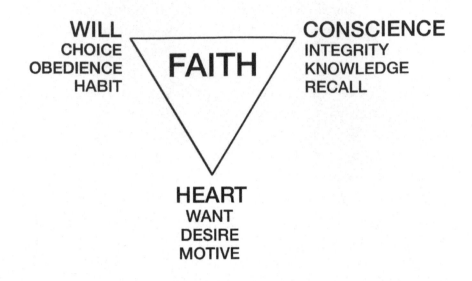

Some say the heart of a person is the spirit of the person, but I don't think that holds up consistently in Scripture. It is true that God gives me a new heart when I receive the Holy Spirit, but it makes more sense to me to see this as a purifying of my desire and motives due to the fact that my old self has been crucified and I have received a new nature—Christ in me. The union of the Spirit of God with my human spirit makes a new me. The indwelling of the Spirit also changes the orientation of my heart, as well as stimulating my will, and enlightening my conscience. It is a reset of my faith clock, if you will. But my heart, my conscience, and my will must be cleansed whenever they are contaminated by sin. My human spirit does not need further cleansing because it is now indwelt with the Spirit of God.

The devil appeals through the weakness of my flesh to try to influence the desires of my heart. My conscience will object by saying this idea is wrong. But if my heart's desire is allowed to give place for the temptation, those desires can grow stronger and try to over-whelm the objections of my conscience with a permission giving **conceit**. Repeated willful disobedience will poison my conscience and could even lead to a moral inversion—where right becomes wrong and wrong becomes right—if this behavior is not repented of.

The heart seems to be one of three components in the determination of my faith or faithless choices. My heart has to do with what I deeply want, what I desire or treasure, and what motivates me (**Matthew 6:21**). It is the place where I believe (**Romans 10:8-11**). It is also the place where I am wounded—where I must heal (**Psalm 147:3**). My heart can become hard (**Mark 3:5**) or soft (**1Peter 3:8**). My heart can be either wicked (**Matthew 15:18-19**) or righteous (**Luke 8:15**) in response to my circumstance or situation. The root of bitterness can grow there (**Hebrews 12:15**). My heart can be cleansed and it must be renewed (**Psalm 51:10**). If my **heart** is determined to sin, it will override my **conscience**. Then my bent conscience will give my **will** permission to sin, through the formation of a **conceit**.

Rhema and The Faith Process

"The Word that is near you, in your mouth and in your heart," quoted above in **Romans 10:8-11**, is the Greek word **rhema**—which is a personal Word of God for guidance in my situation through the Holy Spirit. **Logos** is the Greek word referring to Scripture and makes the same appeals to everyone who will read it. But, the word **rhema** in this verse expresses an intimate and personal appeal to the integrity of my conscience as a child of God—to Christ in me. This brings revelation knowledge to my mind and motivation to my heart. The Holy Spirit is convincing me of what is right in my conscience, to bring me into integrity in my believing. The Holy Spirit is also inspiring the desires of my heart to change, so that my will can choose to obey.

Matthew 4:4 says:
> "Man shall not live by bread alone, but by every word [**rhema**] that comes from the mouth of God." – ESV [Shank]

The Word is near. The Spirit is deeply involved with me. If I am not a believer, He is urging me to repent and be saved by my confession of faith, *taking action* with my will—beginning with the lips of my mouth—that the Holy Spirit may come into me. If I am already a believer, He is urging me to *act like* one by confessing who I am in Christ, and by acting in accordance with that truth—to make decisions to act *as if* the Word of God is true, not from how things may seem or feel to my soul. The choice to act *as if* the Word of God is true is real faith. When I act *as if* what God says I can do, God will take me—by empowering me in my decision to bear righteous fruit.

The evil one is also near whether I am a believer or not. He is making his appeals to bend the integrity of my conscience away from God. He is trying to bend the desires of my heart away from God's desires, that my will would choose to disobey, confess lies with my lips, and remain under his evil power.

If I am a believer, Satan wants to discredit the integrity of my conscience and the integrity of my testimony with sin and a moral collapse. Then in disgrace, I will not be able to bring hope to others in Christ because my testimony is ruined. Satan wants to bend my actions to look *as if* the Word of God is not true. If I obey the evil one by acting *as if* what he says is true, Satan will take me for a ride and I will bear his evil fruit, till I repent.

All this is most dramatically displayed in relapse—when coming out of addiction or other besetting sin behaviors—if I fall back into the old ways. But sin consequences can bring pain that speaks louder than the words the Spirit has been trying to tell me if I have been resistant to hear Him. So, when I finally break down and repent and give myself completely back to the Lord, He rebuilds me by His Spirit and I am now restored in Christ. I testify to my skeptical family and friends that I have repented. I have a wonderful season of sobriety. Some of those who know me may even start to trust me again. But if I relapse, what happens? What is wrong with me? Did God fail me? Am I a hopeless fraud?

Romans 7:15-17 says—in the present tense:

> For I do not understand my own actions. For I do not do what I want, but I do the very thing I hate. Now if I do what I do not want, I agree with the law that it is good. So now it is no longer I [my new spirit nature in Christ] who do it, but sin that dwells within me. [my flesh] – ESV [Shank]

The answer is: I believed that what my **flesh** wanted to do was what I wanted to do. In doing so, I let Satan-as-me act out to bear his sinful fruit. But I must believe the real me is Christ-as-me—here to bear His righteous fruit. My flesh is mine, but it is not me. By the Spirit I am to bring my flesh into submission. If I fail, I am responsible for the consequences.

Have I done these kinds of things? Yes. Is this the real me? If I identify with my flesh, I am hopeless. Then hopelessness takes me. But if I identify with Christ Who is in me, I can overcome if He is really in me. *In Christ my flesh is mine, but it is not me.*

The Opiate of Passivity

Jesse Penn-Lewis has said in the unabridged version of her book *War on the Saints,* that the will is "the helm of the ship." A Free Will is the sovereignty of being each of us is intended to have who are made in the image of God. God is free to choose. He has made us to be like Him in that way. There is no justice without free will to choose—and no righteous judgment either. Those whom He foreknew [would believe] He predestined to be sons. (**Romans 8:29**) For God to know in advance who will choose Him is not the same thing as causing a person to believe or disbelieve. Otherwise, there is no virtue in faith.

We are called to believe, obey, and follow Him. We are called to determine, choose, and act. Passivity of mind leads to dim wittedness, laziness, and distracted thinking. Passivity of reason and judgment leads to a closed mind. Passivity of conscience leads to moral decay. Passivity of spiritual discernment comes from failure to pursue the Scriptures for understanding, and failure to live by what the Word says. Passivity opens the will to being easily mislead by evil into foolishness through lack of spiritual sensitivity and appeals to the sensational. This is going to the flesh by default.

Ephesians 4:19 says:
> Having lost all *sensitivity,* they have given themselves over to *sensuality* so as to indulge in every kind of impurity, and they are full of greed. - NIV

Christ leads through willing participation. He respects my need to reason things through. Satan hijacks my reason and drives me with

72

obsessive desires—creating atmospheres of compulsive sensuality and emotionality—to override my passive will.

The Progress of Corruption:

1. Temptation pulls at the weakness of my flesh and appeals to the self-interest of my soul, apart from my spirit. I should not take condemnation for that struggle, but let my spirit take the lead in what I choose to do. This condition is not yet sin. My flesh will always be whining and fussing to get its way.

2. As Norman Grubb has said, "what you take, takes you." When I choose to allow my heart motivation to bind with temptation, a perverse corruption begins to contaminate my heart with a mindset to rationalize evil deeds. I am now in sin.

3. This heart-motive *binding with sin* brings me under the power of lies. What is wrong starts to seem right or at least justifiable. Jesus said that if I am angry with someone, I have committed murder in my heart. If I am lustful, I have committed adultery in my heart, even if I redirect myself so I do not actually commit murder or adultery, but still harbor the desire. Out of the abundance of the heart, the mouth speaks. In the binding of my heart's motive to hold on to sin, I have deceived myself and my heart is now wicked. The longer I go without repenting, the longer I am deceived. I am now forming a **conceit.**

4. The longer I am deceived the more I will rationalize my behavior with more lies. Spiritual blindness, deafness, and hard-heartedness will then block the voice of God as well as the appeals to my conscience through other believers. My faith can become increasingly subverted and misdirected, and my attitude can become more and more hostile to God.

5. Willful disobedience unchecked by repentance can make a shipwreck of my faith. Without deep repentance, I can even be led to falling away from faith, trampling on the Blood of Christ, outraging the Holy Spirit, and potentially becoming impossible to be restored!

Hebrews 6:4-8 says:

> For it is impossible, in the case of those who have once been enlightened, who have tasted the heavenly gift, and have shared in the Holy Spirit, and have tasted the goodness of the word of God and the powers of the age to come, and then have fallen away, to restore them again to repentance, since they are crucifying once again the Son of God to their own harm and holding him up to contempt. For land that has drunk the rain that often falls on it, and produces a crop useful to those for whose sake it is cultivated, receives a blessing from God. But if it bears thorns and thistles, it is worthless and near to being cursed, and its end is to be burned. – ESV

I have security in the goodness of Christ my keeper, but His keeping is not unconditional. I must persevere in faith and not reject repentance out of contempt towards my Lord.

What I have been describing as stages of corruption through a hardening of heart should provoke fear. The fear of the Lord is clean. **(Psalm 19:9)** The fear of the Lord is clean, enduring forever... **(Proverbs 1:7)** Mercifully, God disciplines me with the correction of consequences. Since a wicked heart can no longer be appealed to with the higher motives of spirit or the love of God—because I am living like one who has never believed—the Lord starts to use consequences to appeal to the self-interest of my soul. This is intended to cause me to want to change my heart, at first only for the sake of myself. (*Ah Lord God, my pleasure seeking has caused* me *to miss true rewards... My bitterness has caused* me *to lose friends... My fears have caused* me *to miss great opportunities...*)

At this stage, I have become like an unbeliever who only wants to save himself from his circumstances. The prodigal son first saw it was not in the self-interest of his body and soul to feed pigs for strangers who hardly fed him. He went back home for the food and shelter. His father took it from there. Most of us came to God to escape the consequences of hell, or to seek healing, or for deliverance. God knows the old sinful nature is not capable of more than enlightened self-interest (*You do this for me and I will do that for you*). The Father gives a whole new nature to those who receive His Holy Spirit and are saved. Higher motivation is not possible without the Holy Spirit in me.

But willful disobedience makes a believer produce the fruit of an unbeliever. In disobedience, I will have allowed my conscience to be numbed with rationalizations, excuses, and even doctrinal perversity about the character of God. A hardened heart seeks doctrines that give permission to sin in areas I do not want to give up. I become blind until I repent and once again return to the Lord. In repentance, what I have now retaken, also takes me back.

Logos and Rhema

To maintain a clean heart, I must have a clean conscience. My conscience must be informed by the **logos** of Scripture as to what is true or the Holy Spirit's personal **rhema** Voice as to what specific guidance I must follow. If there is any conflict between what I believe to be **rhema** and **logos**, Scripture (**logos**) always rules. As we have just seen, my human conscience can be corrupted and the self-interest perceptions of my soul can be deceived by Satan through the weakness of my flesh.

ASSIGNMENT

Whatever I may profess to be my faith, what I do over and over says more about what I may actually believe. Wrong believing becomes a permission giving **conceit**. What **conceits** gave me permission to alter my morality in order to act in those sinful ways?

Column 5 on the Shame Inventory Chart: WHAT DID I WRONGLY BELIEVE ABOUT ME? The information below is offered to help you see actions and motives that may apply in your process. Use whatever may apply as you write your responses to each shame event in **Column 5** on your sheets.

FOR EXAMPLE: I deserve what I took from you against your will. I will make my husband or boyfriend suffer because of what men have done to me. I will make my wife or girlfriend suffer because of what other women have done to me. I know what you need from me but I'm not going to give it to you. You owe me so now you're going to pay. You need to hurt like I hurt. Nobody does what you did to me and gets away with it. Life has not been fair to me so I don't have to be responsible. If I admit I'm wrong, you will hold it over me. I'm a victim so you have to coddle me. Finders keepers; losers weepers. Evil for evil. Dirty for dirty. Curses for curses. I'm the one who should be in charge. I am a completely misunderstood genius. No one understands my special circumstances. I am worthless. I am the greatest. I am the worst. I am helpless and should be excused from responsibility. I am bottomless in my need. I am hopelessly corrupt or defective. I cannot change. I am all alone. I have to be in control. I really don't care what happens to you. I don't have to apologize to you because it will make me look wrong. I don't have to thank or honor you because you will look like a better person than me. *Take notice where some of these conclusions are repeated in your list.*

Column 6 on the Shame Inventory Chart: HOW WAS GOD'S TRUTH CORRUPTED? What lies about God's character and motives were given plausibility by sinful deception?

FOR EXAMPLE: God is against me. God is too strict and unfair. God is not there. God does not love me. I am beyond God's forgiveness. God does not see or care what I am doing. God does not care what other people are doing to me. It is all God's fault. God made me defective. The Blood is not enough for me. God doesn't keep His promises. God is not worthy of my worship or obedience. Faith in God is foolish and without joy... *Take notice where some these conclusions are repeated in your list.*

5

Right Believing
*Lord, teach me to believe and learn to move in my healing, and to
know I am whole and complete and lacking nothing in You.*

My Wholeness and Healing in Christ
If the father I had *wounded* and *disappointed* me, it may be difficult for me to see my new Father, God, as someone safe for me to
love or trust. Some of us came from terrible families. Why did God
give me such wicked parents? How could I be in God's plan when I
was not provided for, or even wanted? The following is a song I
wrote from **1 Corinthians 15: 35-54.**

Sowing & Reaping
When you sow, you don't plant the body that will be
You sow the seed, you sow the seed
God gives it the body that we will see
Each body has its own glory, glory

The sun has one kind of splendor, the moon another
And the stars differ in splendor, one from the other

Heavenly and earthly bodies of wonder
Like the splendor of a sister and a brother

Sown to die but raised up to live
Sown in dishonor but raised in glory to give
Sown in weakness but raised in power without sin
Sown in the natural but raised in the spirit to Him

What is born in the flesh is flesh and will die
What is born of the Spirit of Christ will forever be alive
But the natural must put on the spiritual by and by
The mortal must put on immortal Christ, put on Christ!

When you sow, you don't plant the body that will be
You sow the seed, you sow the seed
God gives it the body that we will see
Each body has its own glory, glory
(*from the album:* PATHOS & ETHOS *by John Byron Shank*)

Look at the wonderful truths in these words. Some of us came from loving and caring families. Some of us were conceived when our parents were in a state of intoxication, some because of moral weakness or promiscuity. Some of us were conceived by adultery, or even rape. Some of us were abandoned by our fathers or even abused. Some of us have never known our natural parents. All of us have suffered and our suffering matters. The choices our parents made matter. Our choices matter too. *But the way my seed was sown does not have to mean I cannot rise above it.* Who you are in the natural would not be possible if you were not the issue of your natural parents—even if they were wicked! God wanted you to BE. And the Scripture promises there will be a wonderful, eternal healing in heaven for those who **put on** Christ and **put off** the sinful *man of dust* to become a new creation in Christ.

The Lord gives us grace where our sins abound and for our weaknesses when they cause us to fall. So we must also give grace to Him when we don't understand why He does what He does. He alone is righteous in all He does. Our grace to Him must be to trust Him in the billions of things He is always doing in the economy of His purpose, for the ultimate good of all. We will understand later what we do not know now.

Reckoning

Many of us have heard of the **Judgment Day** or the **Day of Reckoning**. This is the Day when our lives will be presented before the Lord. The Judge of all the earth will decide whom He will receive into paradise, and whom He will not. **Romans 4:7-8** says:

> Blessed are those whose lawless deeds are *forgiven*, and whose sins are *covered;* blessed is the man against whom the Lord *will not count* his sin. – ESV

A reckoning is a *counting* of what we have or lack. It is also a navigational term. A sailor sets his course reckoning by the North Star. He *counts* the degrees of his compass by it and *sets his direction.* So are we to do in Christ. **Romans 6:1-14** says,

> What shall we say then? Are we to continue in sin that grace may abound? **By no means!** How can we who died to sin still live in it? Do you not know that all of us who have been baptized into Christ Jesus were baptized into His death? We were buried therefore with Him by baptism into death, in order that, just as Christ was raised from the dead by the glory of the Father, we too might walk in *newness of life.*

> For if we have been *united* with Him in a death like His, we

shall certainly be *united* with Him in a resurrection like His. We know that our *old self* was crucified with Him in order that the body of sin might be brought to nothing, so that we would no longer be enslaved to sin. For one who has died has been set free from sin. Now if we have *died with* Christ, we believe that we will also *live with* Him. We know that Christ, being raised from the dead, will *never die again;* death no longer has dominion over Him. For the death He died He died, to sin, once for all, but the life He lives He lives to God. So, you must also consider [*count or reckon*] yourself dead to sin and alive to God, in Christ Jesus.

Let not sin therefore reign in your mortal body, to make you obey its passions. Do not present your members [**body parts**] to sin as instruments for unrighteousness, but present yourselves to God as those who have been brought from death to life, and your members to God as instruments of righteousness. For sin will have no dominion over you, since you are not under law but under grace. — ESV [Shank]

I used to be frustrated with the parts of this passage that say I was baptized into His death—that I somehow died with Christ. How could I have died with Him 2000 years ago? Now I see it. When I received Him into me, I was also received into Him Who died, way back then. If that is true, I will rise from the dead in Him when this mortal body passes away. But even now, I can pray from the Right Hand of God in Jesus' Name!

No longer being under the **law** means my sins are no longer *counted,* as was said above in **Romans 4:7-8**. This means I have the **grace** to learn how to overcome my *old way* of *seeing* myself, and my *old way* of *believing,* and my *old way* of *doing!*

The Word That Does Not Lie

Psalm 12:6 says:

> The words of the Lord are flawless,
> like silver refined in a furnace of clay,
> purified seven times. – NIV

Satan uses trials to harm us. God uses trials to refine us. **Genesis 50:20** says:

> You intended to harm me, but God intended it for good to accomplish what is now being done, the saving of many lives. – NIV

When I took a metal casting class in Art School as a young man, I found the pouring day to be fascinating. The molten bronze being poured into the mold was unbelievably hot. At the boiling point, the dross—the systemic imbedded impurities—rose to the top of the mold and could be scraped off with a hoe. When the metal cooled, the impurities were gone. Our trials bring us to the boiling point. The imbedded impurities of sin and unbelief begin to come to the top. We look bad and we feel bad. Satan wants us to react in despair, fear, or anger. But God is exposing where we need to be purified. When we see our sin and confess it in repentance, we receive revelation and deeper purifying in our hearts. The Word of the Lord has been tested many times over—and is proved to be **flawless**.

The following are faith conclusions based on the Word to which I am now to **reckon** myself in Christ:

The Scripture says I am to **reckon** myself dead to sin and alive in Christ. **(Romans 6:11)**

I am to **act** *as if* I am no longer a slave to sin when tempted, but a slave to righteousness. (**Romans 6:18**) His fruit will follow my faith **action**. This is not fake-it-till-you-make-it because I am standing on Biblical Truth, though my soul feelings may doubt. But by making a faith choice I take *action as if* something is true, whether I feel it or not.

I am to **choose** to see myself as *a vessel* that now contains Christ and no longer Satan. I serve the one I obey. (**Romans 6:16**) I have never been the master of myself.

God is the **Only Autonomous Being** in the Universe. (God is dependent on no one.) The Father, the Son and the Holy Spirit are God. They are the only Eternal and Uncreated Beings. The Godhead alone can *call into being that which is not.* (**Genesis 1 & 2**) All other beings were created by, and are dependent upon, Him for their existence whether they are good or evil.

I am *not the originator* of either good or evil, but by my **choices** I express the will of the one I obey. What I take takes me. The one I obey is the master of my choice and I bear the fruit of the one I obey. If I have sinned, repentance restores me to being able to bear Christ's fruit again. (**Jeremiah 15:19**)

I am to no longer regard myself according to my *flesh* and its desires, but according to my **spirit**, which is *joined to* the Spirit of Christ. At first, this will mean I must choose against my life's history of sin habits, in order to start generating a new history of faith. But this will create a new *normal* for me over time. I am now able to bear His fruit because I am joined in union with Him. (**2 Corinthians 5:16,17 & 1 Corinthians 6:17**)

Galatians 2:20 says:

> I am crucified with Christ: nevertheless I live; yet not I, but Christ liveth in me: and the life which I now live in the flesh I live by the faith of the Son of God, who loved me, and gave himself for me. - KJV

My *old self* has been **crucified** with Christ. It is no longer *I alone* who lives, but Christ Who lives in me—*as a whole new me.* And the life I now live in the flesh I live by the faith **of** the Son of God, Who loves me and gave Himself for me. The faith of the Son of God is now upholding my faith. He is my Rock. Most modern translations mistranslate this passage to say I now live by faith **in** the Son, but the Greek says **tou** which means **of**, not **en** which means **in**. To say I am to have faith *in* Christ is also true, but in this passage the preposition is **of**, not *in.* This means the faith **of** the Son Himself is the ground of my faith.

I am learning to recognize my soul's *self-interest opinion* for what it is, and learning to let my **spirit** decide what I will do. I am *learning* more and more not to live by impulsive thoughts and feelings, but by the obedience of faith, *learning* to live spontaneously free, in Christ.

I'm *learning* to believe I am **seated** at the Right Hand of God in Christ. All powers and principalities are under Jesus' feet, and I am in His "lap". **(Ephesians 1:20 - 2:7)**

The Blood of Christ lets me approach God with **boldness** and without shame. **(Ephesians 3:11,12)** I can let the Holy Spirit *plow my fallow ground* to improve my fruitfulness. He will unmask the **conceits** Satan planted and cultivated in me when I was still his, which may still operate as *habits* to sabotage my fruitfulness, and my witness in Christ.

I have **given** myself to, and have been **received** by God, and I have **received** the Spirit of Christ in my spirit. There are times when the Holy Spirit lavishes His **joy** all over me in worship or in worshipful study of His Word.

I also **trust** that when I *need* a manifestation of His Presence, He will give it to me. When there are no outward manifestations, I no longer *doubt* His Presence is with me because I know Scripture says He is **in** me, to strengthen me to walk by faith and not by sight.

He knows me because He is living out **through** me and **in** me. He experiences me from the *inside* and I experience Him inside me, as well as from above. He knows my heart and He is showing me His because I am one with the Father as the Son is one with Him—and They are to be one with me. (**John 17:20-23**)

Most of us see God as *transcendent*, as high above and distant. He is above and beyond, to be beseeched that His manifestations may come down to us. There is truth to this. But it is also true for the born-again believer that He is now also *immanent*. This means He is as near as near can be, through His Spirit union with me in my human spirit.

I am learning to **expect** that He will work through me at any time. I am my Beloved's and He is mine! (**Song of Solomon 6:3**)

The areas where I still need to *grow* are in my **soul**, where Satan will still try to fool me through my soul's subjective, self-interest perspective. But my **spirit** has been *made perfect* because the Perfect

One has filled my spirit. My **flesh** is hopeless and will be destroyed. I will receive a new resurrection body that will live forever, in the next life.

Column 7 on the Chart: WHAT IS THE BIBLICAL TRUTH?
In order to answer the lies in columns 5 and 6 with Scripture verses that give a new foundation for truth, I have provided a lot of examples for you to draw on below. Because you may not know where to find answers for THE BIBLICAL TRUTH, I have provided numerous verses for you to use where appropriate on your chart. Feel free to stitch them into your process.

The Truth About Me

The following are examples of what the Word says is true about me if I am a child of God. You may use whatever verses below which may apply to your chart in **Column 7** regarding the Truth About Me.

2 Corinthians. 5:16,17 says about right believing:
> From now on, therefore, we regard no one according to the flesh. Even though we once regarded Christ according to the flesh, we regard Him thus no longer. Therefore, if anyone is in Christ, he is a **new creation**. The old has passed away; behold, the new has come. – ESV

1 Corinthians 6:17 says about my unity in nature with God:
> But he who is joined to the Lord becomes **one spirit** with Him. – ESV

1 John 3:2 says <u>I am in God's family</u>:

> Beloved, we are God's **children** now, and what we will
> be has not yet appeared; but we know that when He ap-
> pears we shall be **like** Him, because we shall see Him as He
> is. – ESV

Romans 8:17 says <u>God is my new Father</u>:

> The Spirit Himself bears witness with our spirit that we are
> **children** of God, and if children, then heirs—heirs of God
> and fellow heirs with Christ, provided we suffer with Him
> in order that we may also be glorified with Him. – ESV

2 Corinthians 4:7 says <u>I have a treasure in me</u>:

> But we have this **treasure** in jars of clay, to show that the
> surpassing power belongs to God and not to us. – ESV

John 15:5 says <u>I am joined to Christ</u>:

> I am the Vine; you are the branches. Whoever abides in Me
> and I in him, he it is that bears much fruit, for apart from Me
> you can do nothing. – ESV

1 Corinthians 6:19 says <u>I have the Spirit of God in me</u>:

> Or do you not know that your body is a **temple** of the Holy
> Spirit within you, whom you have from God? You are not
> your own... – ESV

2 Peter 1:3-4 says <u>I have a new holy nature in me</u>:

> His divine power has granted to us all things that pertain to
> life and godliness, through the knowledge of Him Who
> called us to His own glory and excellence, by which He has
> granted to us His precious and very great promises, so that

through them you may become partakers of the **divine nature**, having escaped from the corruption that is in the world because of sinful desire. – ESV

Revelation 1:6 says <u>I have power to intercede for others</u>:
"and made us a kingdom, **priests** to His God and Father, to Him be glory and dominion forever and ever. – ESV

Ephesians 2:6-7 says <u>I sit at the Right Hand above all powers</u>:
"and raised us up with Him and seated us with Him in the heavenly places **in** Christ Jesus, so that in the coming ages he might show the immeasurable riches of His grace in kindness toward us in Christ Jesus. – ESV

Ephesians 1:4-6 says <u>God foreknew I would believe</u>:
"even as He chose us in Him before the foundation of the world, that we should be holy and blameless before Him. In love He **predestined** us for adoption to Himself as sons through Jesus Christ, according to the purpose of His will, to the praise of His glorious grace, with which He has blessed us in the Beloved. – ESV

1 John 4:17 <u>says I am able to be Christ to others</u>:
By this is love perfected with us, so that we may have confidence for the day of judgment, because as **He is** so also **are we** in this world. – ESV

Romans 8:37 says <u>I am empowered to be an overcomer</u>:
No, in all these things we are more than **conquerors** through Him who loved us. – ESV

Galatians 2:20 says <u>I now can live by the power of Christ in me</u>:
I am crucified with Christ: nevertheless I live; yet not I, but Christ liveth in me: and the life which I now live in the flesh I live by the faith of the Son of God, who loved me, and gave himself for me. – KJV

Matthew 5:14 says <u>God's light can now shine out through me</u>:
You are the **light** of the world. A city set on a hill cannot be hidden. – ESV

The Truth About God

Feel free to look up the actual verses I have summarized below. You may use any of these verses that may apply to your chart in **Column 7** regarding the Truth About God.

2 Chronicles 16:9 says:
God knows all. The Eyes of the Lord run to and fro throughout all the earth.

All of Psalm 139 says:
God knows me intimately.

Proverbs 3:19-20 says:
By wisdom and knowledge God founded and established the earth and the heavens.

Isaiah 29:15 says:
God sees the dark deeds we try to hide from Him.

Isaiah 42:9 says:
> What He declared before has happened. What will happen He declares before it does.

Isaiah 46:10-11 says:
> God declares the end from the beginning; from ancient times what will be.

Jeremiah 17:10 says:
> The Lord searches the heart and tests the mind.

Acts 2:23 says:
> God planned to deliver up His Son to be crucified according to His plan and foreknowledge.

Romans 8:27-29 says:
> He searches our hearts and knows the mind of our spirits— and those He foreknew He predestined for His purposes.

Isaiah 5:16 says:
> God is Holy And Righteous.

Isaiah 6:1-8 says:
> The Lord is awesome, high and lifted up, and His train fills the temple.

1 John 1:5, says:
> In God there is light and no darkness at all.

Revelation 4:8 says:
> Holy is the Lord Who was, and is, and is to come.

Genesis 18:23-33 says:

> God is Just, His justice is the extension of His Righteousness. He can be reasoned with, and I can appeal to His justice when I pray.

Job 37:23 says:

> He will not violate justice or righteousness.

Ezekiel 33:7-19 says:

> I must be an instrument to warn the wicked.

Romans 2:2-16 says:

> The Spirit of God challenges me to be righteous as He is.

Revelation 16:5-7 says:

> God is righteous in all His judgments.

Numbers 14:18-20 says:

> God is Merciful, giving grace even to the wicked that they may be saved. He is slow to anger and abounding in steadfast love.

Deuteronomy 7:9 says:

> God is faithful, keeps covenants, and is steadfast in love to those who keep His commandments.

Job 33:14-30 says:

> God speaks in many ways to lead, guide, warn, and inspire me to goodness.

Psalm 103:3-17 says:

> The Lord forgives, heals, redeems, crowns, satisfies, and renews...

Isaiah 55:7-9 says:

> The Lord shows compassion to those who repent.

Lamentations 3:22-23 says:

> The steadfast love of the Lord never ceases.

Ephesians 2:4 says:

> With a great love He has loved me.

James 2:12-13 says:

> Mercy triumphs over judgment.

John 3:16 says:

> God Is Love. Sacrificial love of God.

John 17:20-26 says:

> He makes us one with Him as He is one with the Father!

Galatians 2:20 says:

> He is living out as me; my faith is being upheld by the faith of the Son of God.

Ephesians 2:4-5 says:

> God is rich in mercy to me even while I was still a sinner.

Hebrews 12:6 says:

> The Lord disciplines those whom He loves.

1 John 4:7-16 says:
> If I truly love, I am born of God Who is love.

Psalm 25:10 says:
> God Is True And Faithful. The pathways of the Lord are loving and faithful for those who follow them.

John 17:17 says:
> Because the Word of God is truth, I am sanctified in truth.

The Lord keeps all His oaths and promises.

Hebrews 6:10-19 says:
> God remembers and rewards the good I do in His Name.

2 Peter 3:9 says:
> The Lord is not slow in keeping His promises.

1 John 1:9 says:
> He is faithful and just to forgive all the sins I confess.

ASSIGNMENT

Apply any of the verses above, or others you may find yourself, to fit into your chart in **Column 7** on **the Chart**: WHAT IS THE BIBLICAL TRUTH?

6

In Summary

Lord, open my eyes to see the roots and branches of how Satan has deceived me into partnering with him in evil.

Recently I was teaching this material in a class for men recovering from addiction, and a man strongly protested over the need to do these inventories. He said, "I don't need to do all this stuff. I am a Christian and all my past is under the Blood. I confessed my sins. They are all behind me now. All this digging is making me angry and is tempting me to just go out and get high again, to get away from it. I have been forgiven. It is not right that I have to do this, I am a new man in Christ!"

I asked him how long he had been a real believer and he boldly proclaimed, "I received Jesus seven years ago in a Christian rehab facility." Then I asked him how many times had he relapsed since he became a Christian. He hung his head in silence. He had relapsed many times.

The reason we need to do these inventories—even though our sins have been forgiven—is to find out how Satan has had his way with us, so he will not be able to deceive us again, so easily.

We must learn to protect and defend ourselves with deeper truth in the deeper places. We may have cut off our sin fruit, but we have not known how to cut off *the roots and branches of the inner deceptions which still remain.* The reason these inventories provoke temptation to sin again is because they show that old lies and shame are still inside waiting for opportunity to **sabotage** our lives.

Satan may be gone from our spirits, but his *set-up* will remain in place if we don't fearlessly let the Holy Spirit shine His light on what remains to be seen, to bring deeper healing.

I have learned that if I can talk openly about my sin for your sake, I have separated myself from it. Cowards do not recover. Healing is somewhere outside my comfort zone.

Then another young man challenged me. He said, "I already know why I use drugs—and why I like fast women—they both make me feel good, they give me excitement and pleasure. It is as simple as that. I don't see why I have to go back into my history to find somebody else to blame for my problems. I did what I did, my parents did what they did."

But these inventories are not about blame shifting. Satan is all about blame shifting, ultimately blaming God, giving me excuses and justifications to disobey the Lord. He jabs my old wounds to make me react impulsively to the pain. He reaches his hand through the darkness of what I do not yet understand, to trip me. He fools me into buying evil now, so I can pay dearly, later. Satan is the one who wants me to blame everybody else. He also wants to convince me my flesh is the real me—not who I am now in Christ, in my spirit.

Process chains, set-ups, and scripts

As I said in **Chapter 1**, God has designed an amazing mind for me with a storehouse for memories, and the power to reason and analyze. And I have an imagination to help visualize possibilities. My mind also has a capacity to create process short cuts—like automatic computer software application sequences, or apps, for brain efficiency—so I don't have to rethink what I must choose to do from scratch every time I am in similar situations.

Satan subverts my thinking process with lies—his bad code. He hacks into my life with temptation through my fleshly weakness, so I will make a deal with him to get something my flesh wants, but not what God wants me to have or do. My cooperation with the devil undermines my will and conscience, and it corrupts my heart. He deceives me and I make a *deal* with him, which forms a **conceit**. A **conceit** is a corruption of the truth that gives me permission to disobey the Lord—giving me a high reason to do a low thing. A **conceit** contaminates my process of response so I form bad habits of misbelieving. **Conceits** can be "positive" giving me permission to do what is forbidden, or "negative" giving me permission to avoid doing what needs to be done.

John 10:1-6 says:

> Truly, truly, I say to you, he who does not enter the sheepfold by the door but climbs in another way, that man is a thief and a robber. But He who enters by the door is the Shepherd of the sheep. To Him the gatekeeper opens. The sheep hear His voice, and He calls his own sheep by name and leads them out. When He has brought out all His own

He goes before them, and the sheep follow Him, for they know His voice. A stranger they will not follow, but they will flee from him, for they do not know the voice of strangers. This figure of speech Jesus used with them, but they did not understand what He was saying to them. - ESV

Spirits come and go in the earth, the good angels performing errands from heaven, bad ones on errands from hell. But, the only legal way to *dwell* in the earth is through the doorway of birth. The gatekeeper is the Father. When Jesus came to live on earth, He came by the lawful gate of birth. He came as a Man to redeem the children of Adam and Eve.

Satan and his demons climb in over the wall to spiritually ride on the children of Eve. They are parasites who must have a host because they cannot experience or affect the physical world without a body of flesh. A living body is wet. It is made of blood and water. When demons are cast out of a person, they are apparently sent to dry places for a while, where there is no life. They are sent into something that is dead—that has no capacity for sensory experience. They hate that, because evil spirits have come to kill, steal, and destroy, but they are powerless to do these things unless they find a new living host, so they can act out through a person like you and me.

I believe they find their way back to a host to ride, gaining access through sinful disobedience. They establish their influence by appealing to our **conceits** that promise payoffs but, which actually corrupt the heart of their host with a deal. The longer their host stays in disobedience, the deeper the corruption. Without repentance, my spiritual blindness becomes worse and worse, until I can no longer see the truth. They don't care about me—though they will appeal to me as if they do—they just want to ride on my experiences and sensations and use my body as a tool to undermine and harm others. They want to just ride me into the ground till I am dead, and then move on to another disobedient soul. This is why the Lord calls me to obedience.

Obedience blocks evil from having the right to ride and steer me where it wants me to go. Disobedience gives the right of access and influence by evil spirits by willingly surrendering territory in my life to them. Jesus teaches that if I resist the devil, he will flee, but if I do not resist, he will **stay** until I truly repent.

If I am indwelt by the Spirit of God in my human spirit, Satan can no longer live in my spirit. But through the weakness of my flesh, he will demonize me. Evil will always try to appeal through the weakness of my flesh, and to the self-interest of my soul, to bend me back into selfishness with enticing deceptions. For example, this is why evil spirits encourage intoxication, because getting high is mediumistic in that it creates more opportunity for evil to operate through my weakened will and powers of reasoning. This is also why they harass and inspire intense anger and revenge, fearful over-vigilance, prideful ambition, and lust. This is why I believe sexual relations must be sanctified by marriage, or there will be more than two in the bed of pleasure.

Similar shaming experiences create process patterns we often repeat that go something like this:

Trigger› Interpreter› Conceit› False Payoff› True Payoff

- The **trigger** is a provoking temptation to my soul, which kicks off my *learned* response from past opportunities, vulnerabilities, or wounds.

- The **interpreter** draws on my past experiences and makes what just happened *mean something* which may or may not be true. Like, I get an opportunity to gain something from this. Or, I am losing something from this. Or, I am going to be hurt again.

- The **conceit** is a false belief that gives me permission or *justification* for a sinful response by bending my conscience. This is the most dangerous part of the process because it hardens my heart and corrupts my understanding—giving me a high reason to do a low thing. It is a deal I make with evil.

- The **false payoff** is the selfish goal or *agenda* that will be fulfilled by the sinful choice I have made. This is the deceptive appeal that draws me into becoming a fool when I think I am being wise or smart.

- The **true payoff** is the unintended *consequence* which is not what I wanted to happen, but that God allows to check the momentum of my own destruction. Because my heart is hard, I am not listening to righteous appeals to change, directed to my conscience.

1. **What kind of things trigger me?**
FOR EXAMPLE: Rejection, flattery, criticism, success, failure, betrayal, seduction, abuse, injustice, cruelty, painful recall, euphoric recall, romantic recall, triumphant recall, places, things, and situations that remind me of something awful that had been done to me, or terrible things I did to others. Bad dreams about what happened. Fear that puts me on guard. Anger that stirs up revenge. People who look or act like the ones who hurt me. People who remind me of ones I have hurt. Songs on the radio, certain smells, seasons or months of the year. Seeing or hearing fighting and shouting. Loneliness, grief, hopelessness, rejection, humiliation, big mood impulses.

2. **What does my interpreter say this means?**
FOR EXAMPLE: Here we go again. I am in danger. This is an easy opportunity for me to gain something. This is a deliberate insult. This means you don't really care about me. This means you're trying to seduce me. This means you're trying to pick a fight with me. This means you are trying to control me. You are trying to rip me off. This means you are judging me. This is more rejection. This is abuse. This is more failure. This is more terror. You have just betrayed me. You sold me out. I am always the victim. This tasty thing just dropped into my lap. This is more than I can stand, et cetera.

3. **What conceits give me the right to a sinful response by taking matters into my own hands?**
   FOR EXAMPLE: God does not exist so I will not be held accountable. God does not see. God won't help me or fix this, so I will fix it. God does not care about me, so I won't care about what He thinks. God hates me anyway, so I can hate. God has it in for me, so I get to raise hell. God is a fool and will forgive me later, when I repent. God has already given up on me, so I may

just as well live it up. God owes me for what He has let happen to me. God made me weak, helpless and defective, so why try? God lets evil happen, so I don't have to forgive you. God doesn't apologize, so I refuse to apologize. There is no justice, so I'll be the judge. You don't give me what I want or need, so I will withhold from you what you want or need.

4. **What false payoff am I looking for?**
   FOR EXAMPLE: To do whatever I want. Revenge. Pleasure. Payback. The last word. Justice on my terms. Satisfaction. I can take what I want and deserve. I get freedom from rules. I get even. I force you to feel like I feel. I deprive you of what you want from me so you see how you like it. I escape from trouble or responsibility. I blame you for everything. Now I have the power. Now I *get to* manifest rage, create episodes of emotional drama, give in to sudden irresponsible impulses. I can ride on obsessive compulsive behavior. I can steal from you. I can sabotage what you are trying to build. Nag you to control. I can hurt men for what a man did to me. I can hurt women because of what a woman did to me. I can hurt people of a whole race because of what some from that race have done to me. I can change my mood through chemically altered escape.

5. **What is the real payoff?** (What actually happens.)
   FOR EXAMPLE: Consequences, broken relationships, loss of trust, loneliness, rejection, divorce, poverty, alienated family and friends, disowning by parents or children, friends weary of me or wary of me, people don't like me, breakdowns in health, more bitterness, more shame, more fear, legal consequences, by making victims of others I become a perpetrator. I often received the self-fulfilling judgment on

myself I gave to the interpreted motives of the one who triggered me. As I judge, so am I judged.

As I mentioned on **page 51** under **Healing and Brain Training**: Most brain activity in the course of a day is carried out by my unconscious mind. Situation number 1 has a *learned* A B C response. Situation 2 has an X Y Z *learned* response, et cetera. The ability of my mind to *learn* is part of God's design, and that is good. Once a thing is learned it is stored in my memory as a solution to a problem. But Satan has contaminated many of my unconscious habits of response with lies that affect my motives, values, and agendas. Willful disobedience is an act by my conscious mind to lie to myself in order to give myself permission to sin. This is an *agreement with evil* and gives the devil access to my life and decision making process. Repeated willful disobedience becomes a learned behavior. This learned behavior becomes a settled pattern of response to triggers, which my unconscious mind now regards as a solution. When the same trigger comes up, my mind goes right to the same solution stored in my memory. My learned behavior becomes "okay" because my conscience has now been dulled. Most of the time I just do what I do without re-thinking what to do. But then, my conscious mind wonders why I do the same stupid or destructive things, over and over again!

To correct my unconscious process, I must become conscious of what is going on in it, and then make a conscious effort to replace the *lies* the Holy Spirit exposes with God's truth. The Holy Spirit interrupts my contaminated process with the conviction of sin. Then He exhorts me to take those unconscious habits into my conscious mind for insight, and learn how to make the righteous changes I need to make. With repeated effort, empowered by the Spirit through my will, I can build a new habit and learn to change.

The old problem now has a new righteous solution. My behavior choices start to improve and I begin to heal by faith in who I am in Christ, together with the faith of the Son, Who is upholding my faith. (Galatians 2:20)

It is also true that some of my destructive learned behavior can come from the trauma of abuse, or post-traumatic stress. In such cases, there may be no original willful disobedience deals giving me permission to sin. But the understandable heightened sensitivity can drive me into fearful reflexive responses that quench my faith in God's power to overcome through me. Sufferers of severe violations of trust at the hands of evil people will find reflexive responses that lead to the formation of *conceits* justifying a wider mistrust of everyone, even the Lord. My chart includes both examples of shame from my own evil deeds, as well as shame I got from the deeds others have afflicted on me. In the end, both situations need to be unpacked in order to discover the ways in which the snake has had his way with me.

It will be helpful to honestly look over your chart to see where reoccurring patterns exist. What reoccurring triggers do you see repeated again and again? What responses do you do over and over? What loops are you stuck in? To summarize your findings, write some sentences like the following examples, using this framework:

Trigger Loops & Loop Breakers

When I *experience* **this trigger**, I *interpret* that to mean **this is what is happening**, so I have the right to **a sinful privilege or attitude** as a conceit, which then gives me *permission* to a **sinful retaliation or way to medicate** as a false payoff—but what I really get are **these bad consequences**, as a true payoff.

There are endless variations of this pattern. Use the following examples as a guide to discover the unique ways deception has
infected your particular response to triggers. What you will notice
is that what the **interpreter** says is happening from the **trigger** is
often reinforced in the consequences we actually get from that mis-
direction of our response. Instead of questioning what the
interpreter is saying (by habit) we stay in a repeating loop of futility. On the other hand, we cannot make a straight line, forward
motion out of our problems if we don't question the interpretation—to see if it is a valid conclusion or not. We must also reject
the sinful privilege to which we feel entitled. Better to humbly seek
the Lord in what we should do about what has provoked us.

The loop breaker should look something like this:
When I experience **this trigger,** I now have freedom to **question
what my Interpreter** says it means, so I have the freedom to respond without a **sinful conceit,** and avoid the **false payoff** and
escape the **painful consequences** the devil had in mind for me.

EXAMPLES: Trigger Loops In Response To Fear
When my soul is afraid, I am tempted to respond to my fear with
the old habits of the flesh—instead of facing my fears with faith.
The classic responses the flesh has to fears are: FIGHT, FLIGHT,
CONTROL, or FREEZE.

FIGHT: emotional or physical violence, temper tantrums, disobedience to rules and authorities, threats and curses, quarreling and
contention, to be reflexively reactionary or contrary, feuding, revenge obsessions, bullying...

A Fight Trigger Loop Example

When triggered by a **challenge**, I interpret this to mean **this is war**, so I have a right to **offensive temper tactics** as a conceit, so I can vent **rage** to relieve pressure as a false payoff, but what I get is **fear and alienation** from friends as a true payoff.

———

FLIGHT: abandoning people and responsibilities, escape into drinking or drugs, promiscuity, romantic or pornographic obsessions, hiding from healthy conflict, hiding from internal honesty and real intimacy, self-pity excuses, or reality distorting panic...

A Flight Trigger Loop Example

When I feel **overwhelmed**, I interpret this to mean I **can't do what is expected of me**, so I have a right to **abandon** the work as a conceit, to **escape responsibility** as a false payoff, but what I really do is **betray** those who really need me.

———

CONTROL: ruthless leverage, excessive demands and loyalty proofs, setting traps and snares, forming a posse to get allies, manipulating opinions, slander and lies, playing the victim to justify, turning the tables when cornered, passive-aggressive tactics, sexual aggression, withholding intimacy, or the futility of perfectionism...

A Control Trigger Loop Example

When I am triggered by a **perceived threat**, I interpret this to mean I'm **losing control**, so I must **regain power**, as a conceit, and be **obsessive-compulsive** as a false payoff, but my friends and associates feel **alienated and manipulated**.

FREEZE: suppress emotions, dissociate, shut down, lose emotional presence, blend in to hide, self-harm, play the naïve or innocent to escape responsibility, parasitically attach to someone stronger, become subservient to evil with self-loathing, let my will go limp...

The Freeze Trigger Loop

When I am triggered by the **need to speak up**, I interpret this to mean I am in **danger of rejection or criticism**, so I need to be **silent as a** conceit, to **keep myself safe** as a false payoff, but what really happens is **evil goes unchallenged**.

Various Trigger Loops and Loop Breaker Examples

Now we must add an answer to our Trigger Loop examples with a Loop Breaker—a correction in our thinking process that can begin to bring real change to the ways we habitually respond. The lies we have misbelieved are to be corrected with truth. The bad code we got from the evil one must be removed.

One struggling with rejection and low self-esteem might say:

When I *experience* **criticism** I *interpret* that **it is an insult**, then I have the *right* to **be defensive** as a conceit, which gives me *permission* to **disregard what you have to say**,—but what I really get is to **stay stuck making the same old blunders**, as a consequence.

The Loop Breaker is:

When I experience **criticism** I have the **freedom to question** what my interpreter says it means, so I have the freedom to **resist being**

defensive, I have the freedom to <u>listen to what you have to say</u>, so I can see if <u>what you say is valid or not—or learn something new</u>.

<u>One lacking the support or encouragement from parents or authorities might say</u>:
When I *experience* **being passed over for recognition**, I *interpret* it to mean I am being **cheated, abused, or discriminated against**, so I have the right to **resent authority** as a *conceit*, which gives me *permission* to **be hostile and rebellious**—but what I really get is **more loss of trust and respect,** as a consequence.

The Loop Breaker is:
When I *experience* **being passed over for recognition**, I have **the freedom to question** what my interpreter says it means. Even if my interpretation is true, God is empowering me to **not return evil for evil**. I have the power in Christ to receive bad news **graciously**, so I will **not sabotage** future opportunities.

<u>One who has experienced trauma at the hands of bullies might say</u>:
When I *experience* **confrontation by a group** I *assume* that **I am being ganged up on and assaulted with no one to defend me**, so I have the *right* to a conceit that **God let me be assaulted when I was young with no one to defend me**, which gives me *permission* to **push God away, shut down, or reject** anyone who looks or acts like those who caused my humiliation—but what I really get is **loss of faith and friends who may be trying to help me**, as a consequence.

The Loop Breaker is:

When I *experience* <u>confrontation by a group</u>, I have the freedom to <u>question my reflex</u> because it may not be what my past trauma says it is. I have the freedom to see that <u>God is not my enemy</u>, Satan is. So I have the freedom to be <u>humble and teachable</u> without judging the motives of people in situations like the one where I was harmed by bullies. I am free from the <u>**prejudice**</u> toward whole categories of people—just because they may resemble the ones who hurt me.

————

<u>One who has been molested by someone once trusted might say</u>:

When I *experience* <u>being paid attention to</u>, I *interpret* that to mean <u>**this is being nice as a con**</u>, so I have the right to <u>resist honest and personal exchanges</u> as a conceit, which then gives me *permission* to <u>push you away</u>—but what I really get is to be <u>lonely and unknown,</u> as a consequence.

The Loop Breaker is:

When I *experience* <u>being paid attention to</u>, I have the freedom to <u>question</u> whether this is a cynical ploy or not. I have the freedom to respond with <u>boundaries without becoming defensive</u>. I have the freedom to <u>be real</u> and make new friends with people I like.

————

<u>One who has history as a sexual predator might say</u>:

When I *experience* <u>sexual</u> <u>arousal by someone</u>, I *interpret* that to mean <u>**I should have this person**</u>, so I have the right to <u>possess by sexual conquest</u> as a conceit, which then gives me *permission* to <u>**aggressively pursue my desire**</u>, but what I really get is <u>offending, frightening, or abusing that person,</u> as a consequence.

The Loop Breaker is:
When I *experience* <u>sexual</u> <u>arousal</u>, this does not mean I am <u>entitled</u> to that person. My sexual expression may be <u>mixed with anger and revenge</u>. In Christ, I can <u>control my desire</u> and resist pulling another into <u>sin consequences</u> with me. I am free to seek <u>help and prayer</u> through a Biblical counselor or recovery group.

———————

<u>One who feels unloved may say</u>:
When I *experience* <u>a lack of attention</u>, I *interpret* that to mean <u>I am not loved by you</u>, so I have the right to <u>disrespect you</u> as a conceit, which then gives me *permission* to <u>not give you what you want</u>—but what I really get is <u>escalating arguments and feuds</u>, as a consequence.

The Loop Breaker is:
When I *experience* <u>a lack of attention</u>, I am free to question whether I am really <u>loved or not</u>. I am free to be at peace because I am <u>whole and complete</u> and lacking nothing in Christ Jesus, even if you do not love me. I can <u>be gracious</u> and love you because of Who lives in me.

———————

<u>One who routinely blocks dealing with his or her own sin may say</u>:
When I *experience* <u>myself making a cruel or insensitive remark to you</u>, I *interpret* that to mean <u>it was no big deal</u>, so I have the right to <u>refuse to apologize</u> as a conceit, which then gives me *permission* to <u>avoid an embarrassing admission</u>—but what I really get is <u>contempt from you</u> because I have insulted you.

The Loop Breaker is:
When I *experience* <u>myself making a cruel or insensitive remark to you</u>, I am <u>responsible</u> for any harm or insult I have done to you. I am free to <u>humble myself and make amends</u>, because you are made in the image of God. With <u>humility</u> my friendship with you can be restored.

———

<u>One whose appearance is sexually attractive might say</u>:
When I *experience* <u>a buzz from flirtation</u>, I *interpret* that to mean <u>this is a vital affirmation</u>, so I have the right to <u>enjoy the attention</u> as a conceit, which then gives me *permission* to <u>be indecisive and squishy with my boundaries</u>—but what I really get is <u>awkward and painful misunderstandings and expectations</u>, as a conse-quence.

The Loop Breaker is:
When I *experience* <u>a buzz from flirtation</u>, this is *not a vital affir-mation*, it is only <u>arousal or flattery</u>. I am free in Christ Who gives me my <u>true value and love</u>. I am free to live by my <u>conscience</u> which is informed by the Word of God.

———

<u>One who suffers from loneliness might say</u>:
When I am <u>lonely for companionship</u>, I interpret it to mean I am <u>unloved</u>, so I justify <u>self-pity</u> as a conceit, to <u>indulge myself and complain</u> as a false payoff, but what I really get is people weary of <u>feeling obligated</u> to rescue me.

The Loop Breaker is:

When I am <u>lonely for companionship</u>, it <u>does not necessarily</u> mean I am unloved, I can <u>reach out</u> to others to do fun or interest-ing activities as a liberty, I can <u>show interest</u> in other people, and <u>be a blessing</u> to them and make new friends.

How to make a Trigger Loop

On pages 116 -118 you will find Trigger Loop and LOOP breaker sentences with blanks for you to fill in. You can also download these sentences for free from my website if you do not want to write in your book, or if you only have the audio version of this book. The address again is: johnbyronshank.com/Books/Free Downloads/Trigger Loop Sheets/Get

1. Concentrate on the **Trigger Loop** sentences only and bring your best efforts to the next class. *Wait on doing the Loop Breakers till the class that follows.* Write your answers in pencil as you fill in the blanks. You will make changes as you share your sentences and gain more insight from your class-mates. Some of us will be better at reasoning through this process than others. That is OK. Do your best. This process is a **skill** to be learned. It also reconciles your chart findings with this book.

A common mistake is to give an emotion as a trigger—*when I expe-rience anger I...* But the emotion was provoked by something. THAT is the trigger. How that trigger is interpreted feeds into the **conceit**.

2. For the class or meeting that follows, use your improved **Trigger Loop** sentences to help fill in the blanks on your **Loop Breaker** sentences. Share those findings with each

other to give and receive feedback. If your **Trigger Loop** is flawed, your **Loop Breaker** won't make sense.

From your <u>Shame Inventory Chart</u> in column **4**, look for similar pay-offs and retaliations. You will probably have at least five or six. Take one of the most common ones and construct a sentence as follows:

- Look at **HOW DID I GET REVENGE OR CONSOLE MYSELF** in <u>Column 4 of your Inventory Chart</u>. This is your **false payoff**, put it on line **4** of the **Trigger Loop** sentence below. (EXAMPLE: *So I get to isolate and drink.*)

- From **MY SHAMEFUL MEMORIES** in <u>Column 1 on your Inventory Chart</u>, choose one of the memory **triggers** that provoke you to do this **false payoff** behavior. Write that memory trigger in line 1 in the **Trigger Loop** sentence below. (EXAMPLE: *No one ever calls me.*)

- What does your **interpreter** say that trigger means—giving you an excuse to justify your **payoff**? Write your answer in line **2**. (EXAMPLE: *People don't like me.*)

- How do I find my **conceit**? It can be either some privilege you think you deserve or a permission giving excuse. Look what you wrote under <u>Columns 5 and 6 on your Inventory Chart</u> for clues: **WHAT DID I WRONGLY BELIEVE ABOUT ME?** or **HOW WAS GOD'S TRUTH CORRUPTED?** Put your conclusion on line 3 in the **Trigger Loop** sentence. (EXAMPLE: *I will always be rejected and alone.*)

- Notice that what your **interpreter** says is happening, is often self-fulfilling in what you receive as a real **consequence**. Write your consequence in line **5**. (EXAMPLE: *So, people don't want to be around me.*

The Trigger Loop Sample we just made.

1. When I experience this **trigger**, ___*No one ever calls me.*___

2. I **interpret** that to mean, ___*People don't like me.*___

3. so I have a right to this **conceit**, ___*I will always be rejected and alone,*___

4. which then gives me *permission* to pursue this **false payoff**, ___*So I get to isolate and drink*___.

5. but my **true payoff** is, ___*people don't want to be around me because I am an angry drunk*___.

Once you have 3 Trigger Loops that work logically,
make 3 Loop Breakers for each.

The Loop Breaker Sample from above

1. When I *experience* this **trigger**, ___*No one ever calls me.*___
(But, my **interpreter** may or may not be right.)

2. How can I correct my **interpreter** if it is wrong? ___*Maybe I don't count my blessings so I don't remember when they call*___.

Or, how can I better respond to it if it proves to be true? ___*I can change my attitude and behavior.*___

3. How can I replace my self-serving **conceit** with God's truth? _My God will never forsake me. I am whole and complete and lacking nothing in Christ Jesus_.

4. What is the true **payoff** for doing what God wants me to do? _By being a giver, not acting needy, or desperate, or isolating, people will want to be around me_.

5. What **freedoms** do I have in my life as fruit from the Lord? _I am free to love and be loved_. And I can seek help with my drinking problem.

Now it's your turn to try this exercise.

Again, GET THE TRIGGER LOOPS RIGHT FIRST BEFORE YOU TRY TO DO THE LOOP BREAKERS. If your Chart is flawed in reasoning, see if the sentence examples from pages **103 – 110** will help.

I recommend spending two extra classes on chapter 6 to make sure everyone figures out how to do this. Some of us have not had much practice at self-analysis. Feedback from each other can help a lot. Expect that evil will try to block you with foggy thinking, or taking offence. You are learning how to rake the snakes out of the tall grass. The snakes don't want to be discovered. The Holy Spirit will help you if you ask Him to.

You can download extra worksheets from: johnbyronshank.com/Books/Free Down Loads/Trigger Loop Sheets/Get It

If after spending two sessions on these sentences some confusion remains, and some cannot yet do it, move on through the rest of the book. You can come back later to your sentences. We are learning a new skill that will take practice.

Chapters 7-9 deal with strongholds of contempt, unforgiveness, and making needed amends. Taking action in these areas can break patterns of controlling blindness the enemy has used to keep us disconnected from God's truth in our thinking.

The Trigger Loop 1

1. When I experience this **trigger**, _____

2. I **interpret** it to *mean*, _____

3. so I have the right to this **conceit**, _____

4. which then gives me *permission* to pursue this **false payoff**,

_____

5. but my **true payoff** is, _____

The Loop Breaker 1

1. When I *experience* this **trigger**, _____

2. my **interpreter** may or may not be right. How can I correct it if

it is wrong? _____

Or, how can I better respond to it if it proves to be true?

_____

3. How can I replace my self-serving **conceit** with God's truth?

_____

4. What is the true **payoff** for doing what God wants me to do?

_____

What freedoms do I have in my life as **fruit** from the Lord?

_____

The Trigger Loop 2

1. When I experience this **trigger**, _____

2. I **interpret** it to *mean*, _____

3. so I have the right to this **conceit**, _____

4. which then gives me *permission* to pursue this **false payoff**,

_____

5. but my **true payoff** is, _____

The Loop Breaker 2

1. When I *experience* this **trigger**, _____

2. my **interpreter** may or may not be right. How can I correct it if

it is wrong? _____

Or, how can I better respond to it if it proves to be true?

_____

3. How can I replace my self-serving **conceit** with God's truth?

_____

4. What is the true **payoff** for doing what God wants me to do?

_____

What freedoms do I have in my life as **fruit** from the Lord?

_____

The Trigger Loop 3

1. When I experience this **trigger**, _____

2. I **interpret** it to *mean*, _____

3. so I have the right to this **conceit**, _____

4. which then gives me *permission* to pursue this **false payoff**,

_____

5. but my **true payoff** is, _____

The Loop Breaker 3

1. When I *experience* this **trigger**, _____

2. my **interpreter** may or may not be right. How can I correct it if

it is wrong? _____
Or, how can I better respond to it if it proves to be true?

_____

3. How can I replace my self-serving **conceit** with God's truth?

_____

4. What is the true **payoff** for doing what God wants me to do?

_____

What freedoms do I have in my life as **fruit** from the Lord?

_____

7

Sabotage

Some years ago I was in a family counseling situation. The wife said she was very concerned about a hostile power struggle between herself and her husband, and the effects of that struggle on the children. The husband eventually agreed to meet with us. There had been many separations and threats of divorce. After painful discussions of grievances, wounds, and betrayals in their past histories, a contract agreement was drawn up, as the goal for reconciliation. Time was spent with each of them to see what legitimate needs each one had. I also wanted them to see what cruel treatment each one had perpetrated upon the other, which needed repentance.

After over a year of this hard and painful work, the husband agreed to make significant changes and started to do so. But the wife, who had originally initiated this whole process, refused to change in vital areas that had been part of the contract agreement goals. When

I called her on it, she broke off further contact. I was stunned when I realized that she never had any intention to change herself. She was using me as a tool to manipulate her husband to get what she wanted out of him. She wanted his feet to be held to the fire for his sins, not the same for herself. She never really wanted family healing if that meant she had to give up her power to manipulate and wound! She would not give up her contempt.

She derived considerable satisfaction and validation from her posse—a circle of other women who gathered with her to complain about their husbands. The wife was a hardcore gameplayer. If she had willingly complied with her side of the contract and her family had begun to heal, she knew she would lose her blaming rights. This was ruthless **sabotage**. A professing Christian, she threw Christ and her family under the bus to have her own way. The husband played games too, but he seemed willing to stop.

Games and Conceits

In his book *Games People Play* by **Eric Berne, M.D.** the author uses Transactional Analysis to expose and treat these kinds of theatrical tactics. At the beginning of **chapter 5** of his book, he says: **games** are "basically dishonest, and the outcome has a dramatic quality." He also says; "If someone asks for reassurance and gets it, that is an operation. If someone asks for assurance, and after it is given turns it in some way to a disadvantage of the giver, that is a **game**. Superficially, then, a game looks like a set of operations, but after the payoff it becomes apparent that these 'operations' were really *maneuvers*—not honest requests—but moves in a **game**."

The author says his focus is not so much concerned with criminal con-games, but with the "unconscious games played by... people engaged in duplex transactions of which they are not fully aware, and which form the most important aspect of social life all over the world."

The author goes on to reveal other games. A few examples are described as follows:

If it weren't for you... blaming a marriage partner for all circumstantial life short comings. "You ruin my happiness!"

Now I've got you, you SOB... entrapment to prove superiority.

Kick me... or *Why does this always happen to me?...* a victim using injustice in the service of agendas with sinful privileges.

See what you made me do... or *You got me into this...* always your fault, not mine.

Corner... making it difficult for your partner to resist a temptation in an area of weakness so you can justify punishing them, or withhold something they want, in a retaliation.

Eric Berne goes on to reveal many more games as well as tactical responses for those who no longer wish to play them. But my purpose here is to show how games are an expression of **conceits**. A **conceit** is a false belief that gives me permission or justification for a sinful response by bending my conscience. This is the most dangerous part of my process because it hardens my heart and corrupts my understanding—giving me a high reason to do a low thing. It is a deal I make with evil.

Repeating some of the **conceit** examples I said at the end of **Chapter 4**: I deserve what I took from you against your will. I will make my husband or boyfriend suffer because of what men have done to me. I will make my wife or girlfriend suffer because of what other women have done to me. I know what you need from me but I'm not going to give it to you. You owe me so now you're going to pay. You need to hurt like I hurt. Nobody does what you did to me and gets away with it. Life has not been fair to me so I don't have to be responsible. If I admit I'm wrong, you will hold it over me. I'm a victim so you have to coddle me. Finders keepers; losers weepers. Evil for evil. Dirty for dirty. Curses for curses.

I have found that no significant change in my behavior will last without dealing with my **conceits**, because they give legal ground for the Enemy of God—and the Enemy of my soul—to keep me stuck in futility and defeat. **Conceits** act as a tether pole stuck in the ground. The pole rope will allow me a certain range of motion, but the illusion of progress becomes all too obvious when I feel the snap of the cord, when I want to be free from its limits. With the help of the Deceiver, the very **conceit** I willingly devised with him to give me freedom from my conscience actually hinders me from a clean conscience. Shame then builds up inside me. But instead of dealing with the sinful presumption that is exposed to my conscience, the privilege of my **conceit** overrides my conscience. My **conceit** makes it seem better to disobey than to submit to the truth of God.

My **conceits** make manipulative, destructive **game-playing** inevitable. My games will also **sabotage** my recovery. My **conceits** also protect an **idol** I am unwilling to give up because of the false payoff I believe I will lose if I repent. Refusal to surrender my *contempt* will keep me tethered to my **conceits**.

When we resist the Lord we show we have an unwillingness to be humble. Our disobedience then results in humiliation. My besetting sins were learned through practice. Systems of sin are the construct of many willful **conceits**—masquerading as benefits, comforts, or advantages.

Humbling consequences are the mercy of God designed to motivate me to change when all higher appeals to love, goodness, and wisdom have gone unheeded. The rewards of heedlessness are shameful consequences. This is not in the self-interest of my soul, let alone my heart, or the hearts of others around me.

Repentance

A deep and thorough repentance is necessary. If I am a born again believer, I must stop identifying with my flesh as being the real me. I must learn who I am in Christ by making choices *as if* I can do what the Lord says I can do, according to His Word. I am no longer the slave of sin or my emotions. Then I will begin to see my flesh is mine, but it is *not* me. I will begin to overcome through the life of Christ in me. The following verses are from the ESV translation.

Psalm 51:1-3 is very instructive:

> Have mercy on me, O God,
> according to Your steadfast love;
> according to Your abundant mercy
> blot out my transgressions.
> Wash me thoroughly from my iniquity,
> and cleanse me from my sin!
> For I know my transgressions,
> and my sin is ever before me.

Therefore, I name my sins specifically—no generalized basket of confessions—that I may understand them and be thoroughly healed.

Psalm 51:4 says:
>Against You, You only, have I sinned
>and done what is evil in Your sight,
>so that You may be justified in Your words
>and blameless in Your judgment.

O Lord, In Your passionate love for all the people that You have made, my wounds to others have deeply wounded Your heart.

Psalm 51:5
>Behold, I was brought forth in iniquity,
>and in sin did my mother conceive me.

I was born a child of the Fall as all the children of Adam are.

Psalm 51:6 says:
>Behold, You delight in truth in the inward being,
>and You teach me wisdom in the secret heart.

O Lord, You know the hidden things in my heart. I must not try to hide the truth about my **conceits** from You.

Psalm 51:7 says:
>Purge me with hyssop, and I shall be clean;
>wash me, and I shall be whiter than snow.

Lord, please heal my desires that I may be pure in bearing Your good fruit and not **sabotage** Your wonderful purposes and intentions through me.

Psalm 51:8-9 says:
> Let me hear joy and gladness;
> let the bones that You have broken rejoice.
> Hide Your Face from my sins,
> and blot out all my iniquities.

I desperately need Your encouragement because I am weak. Help my heart to rejoice in Your consequences that I may learn from them. Please do not hold my sins before Your Face, or my wickedness before me, or abandon me to the futility of what my sins deserve.

Psalm 51:10-13 says:
> Create in me a clean heart, O God,
> and renew a right spirit within me.
> Cast me not away from Your presence,
> and take not Your Holy Spirit from me.
> Restore to me the joy of Your salvation,
> and uphold me with a willing spirit.
> Then I will teach transgressors Your ways,
> and sinners will return to You.

Father, grant me a willing attitude. Do not throw me away as I deserve. May the testimony of Your lovingkindness to me be encouraging to those who are still lost, that they may find hope for themselves by Your merciful example toward me.

Psalm 51:14
> Deliver me from bloodguiltiness, O God,
> O God of my salvation,
> and my tongue will sing aloud
> of Your righteousness.

David is referring to his **bloodguilt** in the **murder** of Uriah the husband of Bathsheba, with whom he had also committed adultery. All Israel knew, and his example to them as a righteous man of God was destroyed. But sin in my testimony also makes others stumble over my hypocrisy. Even though the Lord has forgiven me, my sin gives others an excuse to reject any exhortation to righteousness I make. They are tempted to scoff at God's grace and turn away to hell, because of my example. Their "**blood** is upon my head" until I own up and repent. May the Lord show me those to whom I need to make an apology and sincere amends. Failure to do so blocks the blessing of **Acts 20:26-27** which says:
> Therefore I testify to you this day that I am innocent of the **blood** of all, for I did not shrink from declaring to you the whole counsel of God. – ESV

Mark 9:42 also says regarding causing another to sin:
> Whoever causes one of these little ones who believe in Me to sin, it would be better for him if a great **millstone** were hung **around his neck** and he were thrown into the sea.
> – ESV

Then, **Psalm 51:15-17** goes on to say:
> O Lord, open my lips,
> and my mouth will declare Your praise.
> For You will not delight in sacrifice, or I would give it;
> You will not be pleased with a burnt offering.

The sacrifices of God are a broken spirit;
a broken and contrite heart, O God, You will not despise.
– ESV

Lord, I know I cannot buy Your forgiveness or justify myself with good deeds. I can only appeal to Your righteousness and mercy. My righteousness is filthy rags. But by Your righteousness, blessings, and power in me, I want to please You.

Sabotage, Narcissism, & Contempt

- When I separate myself from my sin, I am in repentance. (James 5:16)

- When I deny my flesh with sacrifices to the Lord, I make love offerings of devotion. (Amos 4:5)

- But, if I try to give offerings without first being in repentance, I am in sinful **contempt** and my offering is refused. (Matthew 5:23-26)

- If I refuse to repent when I know I am wrong, I am in **sabotage** mode and I become an instrument of destruction, or I relapse, or I suffer a loss of integrity with others. (Romans 1:28-32)

- In **sabotage**, I **sacrifice** to Satan the righteous ways and purposes of God. Healing of myself and my relations with others is then subverted. Long term patterns of **sabotage** result in **narcissism**—a severe disease in my heart, my will, and my conscience—which destroys real faith. (Hebrews 10:26-31)

- Some of the marks of **narcissism** are: lacking empathy for the feelings of others while feeling entitled to privileges no one else should have; hypersensitivity to criticism but enjoying the suffering of others; turning the tables when confronted to escape responsibility; excessive jealousy and control of others; rage storms; fear of exposure; being incapable of self-reflection; being unable to make relationship commitments; saying thank you makes **me** feel obligated; saying I am sorry makes **me** look like less; only **my** needs matter, to name just a few examples.

Contempt Breeds Narcissism

A moral inversion can occur in someone who knows better, when active **contempt** is not addressed with deep repentance. Real repentance removes the tethering pole that restricts how far the love of God can go in me or out through me to others. Contempt toward others shows contempt toward God in His dealing with me. Contempt towards God pushes Him away to let evil replace His holy leading in what I should do. Going for deeper truth in ourselves in order to heal and restore integrity can sometimes cause a **flip** when I come up against deep and hardened **conceits**. A flip can cause much hard won ground and insights to be lost. A flip can even cause me to turn against the very people who have been trying to help me heal. Satan's view of what is going on pushes God's view aside with slander. Professing Christians who flip have not dealt with their contempt.

Narcissists are made, not born. Most of us are not full blown narcissists but many of us have some of the behaviors. Am I showing signs of **narcissism** while at the same time professing faith in Christ? If so, I must pursue the Lord for healing. **Narcissism** is more serious than mere selfishness. It is vital to know it is the expression of a person—Satan, who has made strongholds in my heart. If I am a Christ person, I must learn how to express the Spirit of Christ Who is now joined to my human spirit. **But,** to say, "This is just the way I am" is to identify with my flesh, where there is no hope.

Again, **Luke 16:13** says, I do the will of one of two masters. I will love one and hate the other. It is vital that if I profess to be a Christian, that I repent as soon as I realize I am off track. To refuse to conform to the will of God means I still have idols I am putting ahead of the Lord that will **sabotage**—make a shipwreck of my faith. If I find I am not yet a real Christian after all, that can be easily fixed by becoming reborn in Christ.

If **sabotage** and **narcissism** are part of my ways, I must learn to fight by seeking help from one who can disciple me, and I must learn to have a submissive attitude. It may be a long battle, but it is a worthy fight. And I can overcome in Christ. **But,** if I remain in the lie that I am only what my flesh says I am, I will remain defeated.

ASSIGNMENT

1. Now that you have looked at your sin systems, what are you still inclined to do in disobedience, to **sabotage** the will of God?
2. What idols make you want to hold on to sinful options?
3. Who and what are you hurting through your willful disobedience and contempt?
4. What must you do to get rid of your idols?
5. Are you a real born-again Christian, or do you need to become one?

8

The Forgiveness Process
Lord, help me cut the soul ties to evil which still remain through the wounds from those who have harmed me.

My good friend Bob Hazen has given me the following observation. It sounds rabbinical in its reasoning.

"Let's say that, firstly, I've become addicted to alcohol. Secondly, I just slipped and gashed my arm with a deep cut. Thirdly, a dog is attacking me.

"There are three agents in this story of my life: me, God, and the enemy.

"My alcoholism and its consequences, are a picture of **sin**. I must address my sin issues primarily by **repenting**.

"My wounds, like the gash in my arm and the resulting **brokenness**, are primarily addressed by God through **healing** and guidance.

"My being **attacked** by a dog is a picture of the enemy's trying to pull me down, deceive and discourage—even trying to build strongholds in me. These kinds of things must be addressed by **spiritual warfare**.

"So consider these three dynamics: Sin requires repentance. Brokenness requires healing. Strongholds require spiritual warfare.

1. For my sin, I need **repentance** from the deeds of the flesh. But repentance alone doesn't address brokenness or strongholds.

2. For my brokenness, I need **healing** in my soul. But healing alone doesn't address sin or strongholds.

3. For enemy attacks, I need to do **spiritual warfare** against my spiritual enemy. But warfare alone doesn't address sin or brokenness."

But, shame permeates all three of these areas. In order to move ahead in who I am in Christ, I will need to seek the Lord for systemic breakthroughs. My shame inventory shows how the presence of sin, brokenness, and strongholds have damaged me. I must continue to explore the process of bringing healing to my soul.

Spirit, Soul, and Body/Flesh Review

My **spirit** is focused on God's interests, if I am a real child of God. The goal of my spirit is to please God and to know Him and His will, by the indwelling of the Holy Spirit. My regenerated human spirit, joined to the Holy Spirit, wants to solve problems by the obedience of faith. A spiritual attack is an attempt to create unbelief in me, even though I am in union with Christ. Demons want me to shrink back in doubt, to lead me out of integrity with who I am in my Lord. Satan is no longer in my spirit, but he lies to me through my soul's emotions, to try to gain power and influence over me.

The **soul** focuses on self-interest. The goal of my soul is to satisfy my self-interest and to know myself. My soul is attacked through my self-esteem, giftedness, purpose and being loved... Satan wants to cause my soul's self-interest to become selfish, by seeking opportunity through my wounds, anger, resentment, fear, anxiety, frustration... Since my soul craves value and purpose, things like futility, rejection, and abuse, are wounding to my soul. (See more in **Chapter 2. Sharper Than a Two-edged Sword** regarding soul and spirit.)

The **body** focuses on the satisfaction of my functional needs and to know my world. Attacks come through weakness and needs. My sin-trained **flesh** wants to medicate my obsessions and emotions with sin. It doesn't want to exercise faith or patience, either. The flesh has to do with gratifying sinful needs and desires. The flesh which wants to disobey, and the spirit which wants to obey, are opposed to each other. (See **Chapter 4: Wrong Believing**)

So what am I to do about my woundedness?
Grieve. Look over all you have written in your chart and your trigger loops. Allow yourself to **see** and **feel** the **truth** of what your life has been like. Pray that you may have courage to **see** what you need to **see**, and **feel** what you need to **feel**, and **know** what you need to **know**. The wounds you have received from another are an *outrage* to your soul, as well as an *outrage* to the justice of God. Part of the restoration of power and dignity to yourself comes when you forgive those who harmed you.

Forgiving those who hurt me is:

>   **not** saying what happened did not matter
>   **not** making excuses for the one who hurt me
>   **not** taking all the blame on myself
>   **not** blocking my feelings and memories
>   **not** saying I don't deserve justice

Psalm 129:1-4 says,

>   They have greatly oppressed me from my youth,
>   let Israel say;
>   they have greatly oppressed me from my youth,
>   but they have not gained the victory over me.
>   Plowmen have plowed my back
>   and made their furrows long.
>   But the Lord is righteous;
>   He has cut me free from the cords of the wicked.- NIV

A *furrow* is a narrow trench made by a plow point when a farmer turns over the soil in his field. Into that narrow groove, seeds are planted to grow a crop like grains or vegetables. This is a good and necessary thing for planting. But in the Psalm we just read, the writer uses the example of plowing to describe *deep wounding*. The Plowman is the devil, acting through the one who has wounded me. The long furrows are wounds into which Satan wants to sow his evil seeds. Seeds of a bitter root, revenge, hate, and fear, are sown into me to contaminate my thinking about God and my value in the world.

The devil wants to destroy my dignity and try to convince me that I am nothing. Jesus said the devil has been a liar and a murderer from the beginning. The one who wounded me has made me feel small and weak. Satan wants to inflate what may be legitimate anger from my wound, into a constant anger that is bent on selfish indulgence, revenge, or medication. He tries to get me to use my anger to hurt those around me, especially those I say I love. He wants to use the wound that gouged me as an excuse to be ruthless. He is determined to use what was an outrage to my soul to make me outrageous! As someone has said, "people who are hurting, hurt other people."

Some of our wounds can hurt a long time. I can remember driving in the car with my young son. Suddenly I would jerk in my seat and say, "OH!" My son would react in fear and say, "What's wrong dad?" Then I would answer him, "Snake bites." He knew what that meant. I was having a painful memory of something awful that had happened to me, or something terrible I had said or done to someone else.

Break the power of others to take away your peace and value.

If I want God to forgive me the sins I did to others through Satan's deception, I must also forgive others who have sinned against me by Satan's deception. I am *tied* with cords to those who hurt me through my wounds, and through the vows and covenants I have made with evil, to get revenge. These form part of the justifying **conceits** mentioned in **Chapter 6**. Vows and covenants are statements like, *I will never let anyone come that close to me again... I will never trust authority... I will never again listen to her...* Those emotional cords are also called *soul ties* that keep my heart tied to the one who hurt me, through my wound. When I remember my pain, I get mad all over again as I relive the experience in my memory. This is why Jesus says I must forgive others or God will not forgive me. Because the Lord uses *forgiveness to cut the cords that tie me to the one who* *hurt me*—so that I can begin to heal—just as His forgiveness of me begins to allow me to heal.

Holding my pain gives me an excuse to act out my anger toward others and gives me permission to do things I should not do. My pain can then become the engine of destruction in my own life. Unforgiveness feeds **the root of bitterness** that strangles every relationship, even my faith in God. This misuse of my pain is hurting those I love. It is hurting my children too, maybe hurting them the most. If I stay in the bitterness of unforgiveness, I make a **covenant** with evil to be ashamed because of what my anger has done.

When Jesus taught His disciples to pray in **Matthew 6:9-15**:
> Our Father in heaven, hallowed be Your Name. Your kingdom come, Your will be done, on earth as it is in heaven. Give us this day our daily bread and forgive us our debts as we also have forgiven our debtors. And lead us not into temptation but deliver us from evil.

> For if you forgive others their trespasses, your heavenly Father will also forgive you, but if you *do not* forgive others their trespasses, *neither will* your Father forgive your trespasses. — ESV *Shank*

Even after I became a believer, I hated this idea. I said it was not fair. I wanted my tormentors to burn in hell for what they did to me. But Jesus says in **Matthew 22:37-39** that I must love the Lord my God with all my heart, my soul and with all my mind, and that I am to love my neighbor as much as myself. Love is a verb, not an emotion. I can take action to do a loving thing, even if my emotions are opposed. This is what David means when he offers a *sacrifice of praise*.

God has given me grace to change. I must also give grace to God for what I do not yet fully understand, or the enemy will stir up rebellion in me. Jesus also says in **Matthew 5:44** that I must love my enemies and pray for those who persecute me. This means that if I love, I should let myself feel my enemy's pain in this sinful world, just as when I was an enemy of Christ, He loved me and felt my pain by living and dying for this world of sin. He took the punishment I deserved for my sin before I even repented. He forgave me so I could have the grace to live, grow, and change. So, I must forgive what my enemy has done to harm me, even before he or she repents.

QUESTION: Really? I must forgive people who are not even asking to be forgiven? What about **John 20:22-23**?

> And when He had said this, He breathed on them and said to them, "Receive the Holy Spirit." If you forgive the sins of any, they are forgiven them, if you withhold forgiveness from any, it is withheld. — ESV

ANSWER: But this passage has to do with equipping the coming of the Church in **Acts 2**, to whom is given power and authority to bind and loose, and to exercise authority over evil in Jesus' Name, at the Right Hand of the Father. This is in order to prevail in spiritual warfare. This is redemptive in its intention, to motivate repentance in another through consequences. It is not an excuse to harbor revenge. This is for the apostles, prophets, pastors and teachers, and the government of the elders to exercise. No permission is given to individual believers to withhold forgiveness from those who have sinned against them personally.

1 Corinthians 10:4 says:

> The weapons we fight with are not the weapons of the world. On the contrary, they have divine power to demolish strongholds. - NIV

Alas, if only the church had remained faithful to the Biblical limits of discipline consequences—shunning and excommunication. When Constantine stopped the persecution of the church, he did a good thing. But when he Romanized it, he put the sword of state into the hands of the church. Beheadings, burning at the stake, the Spanish inquisition, and other barbarities done in the name of the church, have to be explained by real Biblical Christians when trying to share the good news to people who use historical church atrocities as an excuse not to believe.

The Reformation restored *Sola Scriptura* to the church that the Bible alone is the authority in all things doctrinal. Good. But Protestant state churches also have bloody hands from the past. My point is that sin and hypocrisy ruin the presentation of the truth. And my unforgiveness acts as a powerful force to corrupt my testimony when I take vengeance into my own hands.

The generosity of Christ was to love us before we loved Him, and to die for us before we knew we were sinners needing to be destroyed. His Blood pays the price of Moral Justice we could never pay for ourselves.

How does the death of Jesus actually pay for my sins?

Colossians 1:15-17 says,

> He is the image of the invisible God, the Firstborn of all creation. For by Him all things were created, in heaven and on earth, visible and invisible, whether thrones or dominions or

rulers or authorities—all things were created through Him and for Him. And He is before all things and in Him all things hold together. — ESV

This means that if we could put all creation on one side of a scale, and Jesus on the other side of the scale, Jesus would weigh much more because Jesus could make *another* world full of people, and *another* and *another*... So, when Someone of that immeasurable value offers His own death to pay the death penalty for sin and fulfills the standard of the justice God intends for the universe, Jesus *more than covers it.*

There must be justice in God's creation or creation will not be good. **Psalm 9:8**

All that is not good and which will not be repented of, must be destroyed to protect what is good. **2 Peter 3:5-13**

All of us have failed at being good. **Romans 3:23**

The goodness of God wants to show mercy without compromising the standard of Righteousness. **John 3:16-21**

Jesus, our Maker, lived a perfect life without sin. **Hebrews 7:26**

His death in our place fulfills the penalty we deserve. **Hebrews 10:9-10**

God declares we who believe in Jesus are now holy and good through the union of His Holy Spirit, in our human spirits. **Galatians 5:16-18**

His Holy Spirit in us makes it possible to begin to learn how to walk in righteousness with the grace to learn from our sins when we get fooled by the enemy. **1 John 1:5-10**

And the Father, the Judge of all the world, accepts the Sacrifice of Christ, and forgives you and me if we will believe and receive the Spirit of the Lord into ourselves. His Power breaks the power of sin that has been destroying you and me. The world to come will be righteous and wonderful *forever.* You and I must be *changed* in order to share in that new world *forever!* To be with *God* is to have everything good for eternity. To be with *Notgod* is to have all that is not-good *forever.*

How does the death of Christ break the power of Satan?

Jesus also said if we break any part of the Law we break the whole Law. The prayer of the righteous is powerful and effective. (James 5:16) So the prayer of the *unrighteous* must be weak and ineffective because God will not hear it. The death of Christ in me *breaks* the power of Satan to argue that I have no rights to God's favor because of my sins, holding God hostage to His Own Command.

I, myself, must begin to break that evil power in me through real forgiveness. What God commands is clear: the one who sins shall **die**. Satan uses that as leverage against me before God, to block blessings from the Lord, if I refuse to repent. The devil can stand before God and say: "Do not answer this man's prayer or show him mercy, because he does not show mercy to forgive others. This man disobeys Your fixed command. You, O God, must not go against

Your Own Holy Words to even hear his prayer!" On top of all that, the poison of anger and revenge, prevent me from healing.

Understanding this, I used to say I forgave those who hurt me, but when painful memories came up, I'd get mad again. And then I would condemn myself because I thought I must not have forgiven them after all. My pain and desire for revenge was still there. I thought I must be unable to forgive! Then a wise older man, named Norman Grubb, set me straight. I was believing what my emotions said, not what my spirit said. He said forgiveness was a spiritual transaction with God, not an emotional one. If I had **done** it, I must **believe** it and **stand** on it, just like when I gave myself to the Lord in surrendering prayer, and He took me.

So what is real forgiveness? Here is a sample of how I pray to forgive someone who has hurt me. Fill in the blanks below with the name of *one* who has harmed you. *Do not name yourself here.*

Forgiveness Prayer - *dropping all charges*
Lord, I release _____ in Jesus' Name. Hold no sin or offense against _____ on my behalf, forever. Open the way of healing, revelation, salvation, and blessing to _____ because I plead the Blood of Jesus for _____ sins against me. Show _____ the same mercy You showed me. May _____ now be able to see, hear, and be healed in Jesus' Name, as You have so graciously done for me.

Then, when those snake bites of painful recall arise in me to tempt me with anger and the desire for revenge, I must answer them like this:

Condemnation Answer

Say to the devil: It's no longer *me* who wants revenge—I am a new creation in Christ. That desire is coming from you, *Satan*, who is trying to get me back into condemnation and unbelief. I refuse shaming condemnation for those thoughts and feelings because they are no longer coming from me, and *God is my witness* that I have released _____ from judgment as far as I am concerned. My emotions are something I am experiencing in my soul, but they are no longer the desire of my spirit. I repent of measuring myself by what my *emotions* want to do. I also repent of justifying revenge by my *pain*.

Remember **Psalm 129:4** where it says:
> But the Lord is righteous;
> He has cut me free from the cords of the wicked.

Those cords are *soul ties* that bind me to the one who hurt me through my memories and emotions. When people who look like the one who hurt me, or places or circumstances similar to the situation I was in occur, I may get triggered. But when snake bites return I must answer them with faith like in the example above. Deeper wounds may take longer, but the more I speak back the truth, the more I will heal. As I do, real healing increases because I am standing in faith.

Imagine you are watching a bull fight. In the ring, you see a huge bull and a skinny little matador in a sparkling suit, waving his red cape at the bull. The fancy matador is the devil. The large bull is the Christian, empowered by the Holy Spirit. The red cape is the trigger to temptation, condemnation, or accusation. The bull could easily gore the matador with his power, but he does not know what *power he has in Christ.* The matador is taunting the bull with painful memories or a strong sinful desire. He fools the angry bull into charging the red cape of painful thoughts and memories, in order to wear him down with obsession and futility. Then, the matador starts sticking lying darts into the bull as he continues to waste his strength in charging the cape. The bull is starting to lose blood in weariness and fatigue. The devil wants to weaken the bull until he can finally kill him with his sword—after he has finished playing with him. In the same way, the devil wants to destroy my faith by keeping me from fighting my real enemy (Satan) with the Power God has given me in Christ.

Only God can forgive all the other sins the one who hurt me has committed. Those sins remain between God and the one who hurt me. Satan was using those people to harm me. Now I must let Christ use me to forgive them. I must freely grant forgiveness to the one who has hurt me, I must not wait till they have earned the right to be forgiven. But I am *not obligated* to trust that person before it is earned. (Forgiveness is granted, but trust is earned.) God did not wait for me to earn His forgiveness. And I am not commanded to be around someone who may seriously harm me again unless they also change and become safe. But I must forgive.

Over the years, I have been amazed to find that my soul and my emotions are healing. My pain from others in the past is now almost completely gone. When forgiveness is given to others, the healing begins. I only have the authority to forgive what they did to *me.* They must deal with God for the rest of their sins as I must deal with God for mine. My wounds and consequences are real. I remember them. But now, I am more and more free from the evil power which came through the pain that others have caused me.

My old wounds no longer have the power they once had to warp my judgment and response. I can continue to heal and grow more and more each day, in the grace God has given me.

Consider the following:

What people or institutions do you hold bitterness against?

What prevents you from releasing them?

How can you deal with the snakebites of painful recall?

ASSIGNMENT

Who do you need to forgive?

What does the Lord want you to do for change and healing?

It would be good to put the name of *one person* you need to forgive in the blanks of the **Forgiveness Prayer** and the **Condemnation Answer** beginning on page **140**. Make the transaction with God to release *that person* in Jesus' Name. As you answer the condemnation from future snakebite attacks, you will begin to heal. Bigger offenses may take longer, but they will heal as you remind Satan that **God is your witness to your forgiving** *that person*. If necessary, you have the freedom to have healthy boundaries with *that person* if they continue to wound you, but you must forgive.

Going forward, I must forgive everyone the Holy Spirit brings to mind, that the favor of God be not hindered in my life.

9

Making Amends

O Lord, make me an instrument of peace and healing as I make amends to those I have harmed.

Secret sin destroys from within.

Luke 12:1-3 says:

> In the meantime, when so many thousands of the people had gathered together that they were trampling one another, He began to say to His disciples first, "Beware of the leaven of the Pharisees, which is hypocrisy. Nothing is covered up that will not be revealed, or hidden that will not be known. Therefore whatever you have said in the dark shall be heard in the light, and what you have whispered in private rooms shall be proclaimed on the housetops." -ESV

These are scary words spoken to *the disciples.* We who believe are also disciples. On the Last Day—that Great and Terrible Day of the Lord—**Justice** and **Truth** will be fully restored and **Hypocrisy** will be exposed. All of us will fall short, but all of us who believe will have our sins forgiven. But many of us will ask, "Why were my prayers in certain situations not answered?" Sometimes it will be because our secret sins held us in unrighteousness, so our prayers were hindered, as a consequence. Sometimes we were called to stand for or to help others, but the priority given to secret sins kept us numb and distracted. Our secret sins made us willfully disobedient. Those we said we loved—who needed us the most—deserve an explanation for why we let them down.

Therefore, it would seem wise to expose our secret sins now. If they are no longer secrets, perhaps there will be no need for them to be shouted from the roof tops. Our secrets keep us sick and we need healing. Our sickness makes others sick and makes them stumble. Our hypocrisy ruins our testimony. Woe to us if others turn away from Christ because of our example.

The inverse property of this principle is that the secret words and deeds which are *righteous* will be openly rewarded in heaven as well. In **Matthew 6:5-6** Jesus says:

> And when you pray, you must not be like the hypocrites, for they love to pray standing in synagogues and at the street corners, that they may be seen by men. I tell you the truth, they have received their reward. But when you pray, go into your room and shut the door and pray to your Father Who is unseen. Then your Father Who sees what is done in secret will reward you. —NIV

So, integrity with God is highly important. Many of us think we can get a full time blessing for a part time commitment. But half way measures avail us nothing. Saying NO to the Holy Spirit grieves Him, and blocks the fruit of the Spirit from manifesting. If I cannot say NO to the devil when he harasses me, why should I believe he will flee my friend for whom I am praying in Jesus' Name?

Matthew 5:23-26 says:

> So, if you are offering your gift at the altar and there remember that your brother has *something against* you, leave your gift there before the altar and go. First be reconciled to your brother, and then come and offer your gift. Come to terms quickly with your accuser while you are going to the court, lest your accuser hand you over to the judge, and the judge to the guard, and you be put in prison. Truly, I say to you, you will never get out until you have paid the last penny.
> – ESV

Psalm 126:4-6 says,

> Restore our fortunes, O Lord,
> > like streams in the Negev!
> Those who sow in tears
> > shall reap with shouts of joy!
> He who goes out weeping,
> > bearing the seed for sowing,
> shall come home with shouts of joy,
> > bringing his sheaves with him. – ESV

The Negev is a dry desert wilderness in southern Judah. A desert like that would be miraculously restored if a stream suddenly appeared in it. Sheaves are the crops to be harvested and carried in the arms of the one who harvests them. Sin has made our lives like a desert—miserable for our families, too. But the streams of Life coming by the Holy Spirit can miraculously restore our suffering families. For this to happen in my family, I must first *humble* myself before God and them. I must *agree* with those who have a legitimate grievance with me. I must give myself time for *real godly sorrow* to come into my heart for the sins I have committed against God and the ones I love. Many of us have had hard and unfeeling hearts, too dull to feel anyone else's pain but our own. Maybe now I am beginning to have some sympathy for those whom I have neglected or harmed. That is progress. But in order to make an effective amends, I must move past sympathy to empathy—letting myself feel what it must have been like for the one I have hurt, to be wounded by me—really coming to identify with what they have lost because of me.

I must seek the Lord with determination to let myself *see* what I have done to another and *feel* the gravity of it. Then my heart will soften and my conscience will be restored to tenderness. Sowing new seed with tears over what I have done to another, in empathy with the suffering I have caused, can bring about the possibility of a new harvest of joy. But I must really change. The Lord must be living inside me for that to happen. It will take time and I must be patient. There are seasons in our lives. *There is a time to plant and a time to reap.* (Ecclesiastes 3:2) Have I not made God and my family wait for me to change? God forgives immediately, but my family may take a while. Some of them may never forgive me, and in such cases I must respectfully learn to live with that, trusting God for a better future. *There is a time to seek, and a time to lose.* (Ecclesiastes 3:6)

Apologies are good for lesser offenses, but they do not have the power for lasting impact like a clean and sincere amends for larger offenses. When I sincerely apologize, I acknowledge I have offended someone. This is good, so long as I'm specific about what I did wrong. An insulting apology makes things worse. It goes something like this: "I'm sorry **if** I hurt your feelings." This only shows concern for myself. I'm just trying to minimize my offense without owning the fact that I have done something wrong. Using the word **if** also implies my offense is not necessarily real or true, or is not really as important to me, as it is to you. Do not use the word **but** either to justify what you did with an excuse. If you do, your amends attempt will be broken with another argument.

- A sin from another that is not forgiven has the power to *tie* my soul to the one who hurt me, through my wound.

- A sin that I have committed that I have not acknowledged, builds a *wall* against me in the heart of the one I have hurt.

An amends is stronger than an apology. It is an offer to restore what was lost, replace what was damaged or stolen, or make a big change in my behavior. I put my own skin in the game. I must stand up and *own* my responsibility. But before I do that, I must allow myself to let the emotional force of what I have done *land on me*. I must let myself see how precious the hopes and dreams are of the ones I have hurt—and what I have done to damage them. I must have a plan for change. I must be humble when I talk to them. I must let them know I now understand how much damage I have I caused. My remorse must be real. I must ask the one I have harmed to forgive me. This is not the time to bring up whatever may be the fault of the other to provoke me. I must just own my side of the street, not theirs. Otherwise things will descend into another blaming argument and opportunity for healing will be lost. But if the amends is accepted, an opportunity to unpack shared blame may be possible later, when and if good will is restored.

Amends to those whom I have hurt is:
>
> **not** saying what happened did not matter
>
> **not** making excuses for what I did to hurt them
>
> **not** shifting the blame on to what they may have done
>
> **not** minimizing the damage to their hopes and dreams
>
> **not** saying they don't deserve justice

Repentance Considerations

How did I specifically hurt each one? (in column 3 on your chart sheets)

What am I going to change in me, to heal and protect those I have harmed?

What must I change in me, to become more loving and responsible?

Bloodguilt on the Land

The Blood of Jesus cancels the power of all my sin to hinder me from salvation and eternal fellowship with the Lord. Blessed is the one whose sins are no longer remembered before the Lord. If I have made peace with God in repenting and being born again, I am now at peace with Him.

However, others against whom I have sinned may not be at peace with me. My testimony of faith in Jesus may cause them to wince and scoff at my hypocrisy, if I have not also made peace with them. At various times the Lord will say to me, "go to so-and-so and make an amends for what you did." When He does that, there will be no peace in me until I do it, there will be a kind of "**bloodguilt on my land.**" As godly remorse grows, the gravity of my offense becomes more evident through the Holy Spirit's conviction. If I ignore the

Spirit, I will continue to have relationship consequences, as well as shame.

A severe example of literal **bloodguilt** is seen in the following passage. Sometimes real sacrifice is necessary for the sake of shalom being restored.

2 Samuel 21:1-9 says:

> Now there was a famine in the days of David for three years, year after year. And David sought the face of the Lord. And the Lord said, "There is **bloodguilt** on Saul and on his house, because he put the Gibeonites to death." So the king called the Gibeonites and spoke to them. Now the Gibeonites were not of the people of Israel but of the remnant of the Amorites. Although the people of Israel had sworn to spare them, Saul had sought to strike them down in his zeal for the people of Israel and Judah. And David said to the Gibeonites, "What shall I do for you? And how shall I make atonement, that you may bless the heritage of the Lord?" The Gibeonites said to him, "It is not a matter of silver or gold between us and Saul or his house, neither is it for us to put any man to death in Israel." And he said, "What do you say that I shall do for you?" They said to the king, "The man who consumed us and planned to destroy us, so that we should have no place in all the territory of Israel, let seven of his sons be given to us, so that we may hang them before the Lord at Gibeah of Saul, the chosen of the Lord." And the king said, "I will give them."

But the king spared Mephibosheth, the son of Saul's son Jonathan, because of the oath of the Lord that was between them, between David and Jonathan the son of Saul. The king took the two sons of Rizpah the daughter of Aiah, whom she bore to Saul, Armoni and Mephibosheth; and the five sons of Merab the daughter of Saul, whom she bore to Adriel the son of Barzillai the Meholathite; and he gave them into the hands of the Gibeonites, and they hanged them on the mountain before the Lord, and the seven of them perished together. They were put to death in the first days of harvest, at the beginning of barley harvest. – ESV

Yikes! That was hard. I don't see the Lord calling us to such measures today. God did so with Himself, in sending His Son to **die** for my sin. But, I must take seriously what I have done to another—even though God has forgiven me. I must try to fix what I can fix, and trust the Lord for what I cannot fix. If I can repay, I must repay. If I am forgiven by the one to whom I make an amends—great. If they say they will never forgive me, then I must humbly thank them for listening to what I had to say, and walk away without arguing. If they say they forgive me but no longer want relationship with me, I must accept their boundaries. If I do, I am acting in good faith. My "land" can then be healed of shame. I will have shalom with God even if I do not have it with those who still count me as their enemy.

Step 8 in the Alcoholics Anonymous Big Book says I am to make a list of all the people I have harmed and be willing to make a sincere amends to them all. (Being willing to fix what can be fixed)

Step 9 says I am to make a direct amends wherever possible, only to those I will not further harm by contacting them again. (Being willing to trust the Lord for what I am unable to fix)

I have made many amends to family members, women I have loved, employers, former friends, and people I turned on to drugs... Most have forgiven me, but some of them refused to forgive me. But whether I was forgiven by them or not, the blessing of the Lord has rested upon me and He has removed a great load of shame from my back.

A Guide for Making Amends – *healing in humility*

When making an amends with small children, a change of behavior may be enough. But the older they get, the more they will understand the ongoing offenses for what they are, and become bitter and distrustful. Adults need a whole lot more from us in order to be convinced. Look at the following example letter and use whatever applies in your situation. This one happens to be tailored towards making amends to an abandoned mother with children.

EXAMPLE LETTER:
I have been thinking a lot about you, as well as how much I have hurt you. I have been very upset with myself for how I have...(*Name what you know this person has against you. Be **specific**—no basket confessions like "I was selfish, or I was an alcoholic."*) Name all that is in the basket. You know the specific things she has against you.

I am appalled at how you were treated by me. I don't blame you for being angry and disappointed with me. I understand how you may not feel safe to trust me right now. You did not deserve this from me, and I understand that you don't want to be hurt by me anymore. I am so sorry.

I know I can't change what happened, and I can't repay the harm I have done to you. I can only hope you will someday be able to forgive me, *not* because I deserve it, but so God can bring healing to your heart for the pain I have caused you.

I want to be a better person. I want to be involved with your life in a way that will show how much I regret what I did to you—*if you will let me.* I want to help you in any way I can, as soon as I am able, as much or as little *as is comfortable to you.*

Notice what is going on here. I know that when someone has really hurt me with a deep wound, I feel like my *dignity, rights, value, and power* have been gouged out of me. I'm left feeling *weak, small, dishonored,* and *abused.* Then the enemy comes and sows seeds of bitterness into that wound. Those bitter seeds intensify my legitimate anger to feel like I have power and rights to revenge. I will try to build walls against the one who hurt me, to keep them out. And, what I call a *frustration feedback loop,* gets set up in me with memories and revenge fantasies recycling over and over inside. Pain and obsession recycle over and over like a microphone placed in front of a loudspeaker on stage that screeches—EEEEEEEEEEE— inside me!

So, when I have really seriously wounded another, I must remember to empathize with them. The same crippling gouge and revenge response that I feel has happened inside me, is happening to the one I have harmed, too. I have created a screeching *frustration feedback loop* in them too! That's why I recommend language that acknowledges the right of the one I have harmed to feel angry, robbed of dignity, safety, or power. My amends should focus on giving back to them some justice, respect, and power so they might once again be able to rebuild trust with me. I must show that **I get it** by humbling myself in genuine remorse.

Showing Throat

Some years ago, I saw a documentary film on TV about a wolf pack. One scene showed a challenge by a younger male to be the new leader of the pack. It was a fight to the death because the winner would have the right of access to the females. The loser would either die or have to flee the pack and become a lone wolf. It would be harder to get supper for a wolf hunting alone. A pack can spread out and outflank the prey they are pursuing—giving them the possibility of a much higher rate of success.

But what was interesting to me was a third option. If the wolf who was losing offered his throat to the stronger wolf, the stronger one would let him live. The weaker wolf would then be allowed to stay with the pack because he acknowledged the rights of the stronger wolf. He would then be able to continue to benefit from hunting as a pack-member, much more than if he fled and had to hunt as a lone wolf.

There is a lesson to be learned here. If I have seriously wronged you, the Law of God is against me if I continually justify myself with excuses, or ignore my offense. The justice you deserve is against me too. You will put up a wall against me to keep me out, for good reason. When I have been in the wrong, I must have the humility to show throat, I must make a sincere amends. This is *not* the time to make any excuses. This is *not* the time to blame you for causing what I did, even if you had a role. I must own my side of the street only, not yours. A clean amends is a straight forward apology and a humble request for forgiveness. Anything more than that will result in another argument.

If I am making an amends to the mother of my child, I want to give her a chance to see me in a new light, as someone she might dare to trust a little. She will not let me near her if she does not feel safe, or if she is still angry or deeply offended. She will not want to let her wall down because she believes she has no reason to trust me again. Sorry is not enough. There must be changes in my life. I must show her *I get it*, and I am grieved over what I did. I must not push her faster than she wants to go. I must give her time. If she feels she is respected, she may become ready to make a small step of trust, to see what happens. God resists the proud but draws near the humble. So do the people we have harmed.

The same attitude applies for a woman making amends to a man. Show throat, humble yourself, be specific. Do not bring up his part in it. If you justify what you did by saying, "You did this to provoke me!" your amends will break down into another argument and more wounding. It will make things worse. An amends must have the attitude of standing before God. He will not accept excuses for my sins based on the unfairness of others. The Lord will hold us all to the same standard He lives by—not to return evil for evil, but return good for evil. **(Romans 12:17)**

Again, I have made numerous amends to those whom I have harmed or offended in my past. *Not all of them have forgiven me.* But the Lord has taken great loads of shame off my back because I did what He asked of me, whether the person forgave me or not. Trying to forgive myself never works. What authority does a sinner have to forgive his own sins, when he first talked himself into doing what he did? I found myself unconvinced when I tried forgiving myself. It was my outraged vanity that was disappointed in me—I should have been a better man. It was earthly sorrow, not godly sorrow. The only ones who have power to forgive are the ones I have harmed and the God I have disobeyed. *When God releases me, I am released from my shame.* I must let the Holy Spirit lead and guide me in how I pray and act. I must not rely on my own natural abilities. Only the Spirit knows what to do and when to do it.

1 Corinthians 2:10-11 says:

... these things God has revealed to us through the Spirit.
For the Spirit searches everything, even the depths of
God. For who knows a person's thoughts except the spirit
of that person, which is in him? So also no one compre-
hends the thoughts of God except the Spirit of God.
Now we have received not the spirit of the world, but the
Spirit who is from God, that we might understand the
things freely given us by God. And we impart this in words
not taught by human wisdom but taught by the Spirit, in-
terpreting spiritual truths to those who are spiritual. - ESV

Amends in Spiritual Intercession – *from Deep Discipling*

Putting all these truths together, we have promises from the Lord
that can revolutionize our faith and reveal amazing strategies in the
Holy Spirit. The Holy Spirit knows all—all of me, all of you, and all
of God. Intercessory prayer is not just a request or a petition. An
intercessor stands before God in the place of another who either
cannot or will not stand there themselves. An intercessor must
identify with the person they are praying for by standing in that
person's shoes, and making an effort to know what it is like to be
that person under the circumstances in which they are living, here
and now. Christ did that by living under what we have to live with
on earth and was tempted in every way as we are. But, even though
He did not sin, He has personal empathy with us—because He felt
the pull of temptation.

An intercessor must also identify with Christ as He is now, at the
Right Hand of God, speaking and acting with authority on behalf of
the one for whom we are praying. With the faith of Christ upholding our faith, we must speak out and believe for the power of God
to cause break-throughs in the heart and circumstance of the one
for whom we are standing.

In interceding for my beloved adult son, I learned that I had to first take a stand against his sin by telling him it was putting his soul in jeopardy. *Right and wrong were clearly defined.* Having done that, I tried to find every other way possible to encourage him. We talked often of things we both enjoyed. When he suffered hurts, I mourned with him. When he had successes, I rejoiced with him. I often encouraged him to faith as far as he would let me. I shared with him my own struggles with sin. (He was an adult at that time, it would be harmful to do make him a confedant, if he was still a minor) I shared my own triumphs and failures. Sometimes he threatened to cut me off when I said something he didn't like hearing, but I remained patient because I loved him, and I knew he loved me.

I also tried to educate myself in the powers of the besetting sins that held him so tightly. There were lies at the bottom of his assumptions about himself. There were also deceptive reinforcements that were the consequence of his disobedience. There were soul ties to fellow sinners. There was shame and condemnation. Of course, I made many mistakes, but I did as much as I could to understand *what it must be like to be in his shoes.* I never judged him for his temptations. Temptation is not sin. I most certainly have plenty of my own temptations. Jesus was tempted in every way we are, but He did not sin.

Clearly, my son was suffering spiritual blindness because of his own sin. Blindness, deafness, and a hard heart are the consequences we all have when we refuse to repent. (**John 12:40**) However, because my son was able to use my sins as an excuse to dismiss my calls to return to the Lord, the Spirit led me to make amends for many sins I had committed against him as his father. Whenever I saw one, I confessed it to the Lord and to my son and asked for forgiveness.

My *sin* had ruined my integrity as a father. But my love motivated me to restore that integrity for my son's sake. It also drove me to repent of how I had misrepresented the Lord. I began to open up more of my process in dealing with my own temptations, from a Biblical point of view. My son knew about my successes and failures. I acknowledged many of my fears and weaknesses as well. Sometimes he used these confessions against me, but so what! This is my son; I would die for him, if necessary.

Over the course of several years I made six or seven amends to my son. I will tell you about one of them. I was praying for him one night and God gave me a memory:

My son was standing near the front window of his bedroom upstairs. I think he was fourteen or fifteen years old. I was extremely angry with him about something and I was blowing fire all over him in my rage. His young skinny frame was recoiling in horror, but what I did not see at the time is what God saw. My son was living without his mother because she had left the family, and he only had his dad, and his dad was *scary as hell right now*. I didn't see his vulnerability at all in that moment. It killed me when I saw it. His mother had left him, and he was living with a father who was now terrifying.

The next morning, I called him. I told him what God had showed me and how devastated I was over what I had been like, and how much I had hurt him in those hard days. I begged him to forgive me. He was silent for a while, then the he softly said "yes." A stronghold of bitterness toward me started to lose power in him when he forgave me.

In receiving that memory from the Lord, and letting it soften more of the hardness in my own heart, I was able to start to heal more in my conscience. In making that amends, the Lord was able to soften more of the hardness in my son's heart, bringing healing to him, and creating opportunity for him to trust in me. Christ was glorified and He was able to restore more integrity to my profession of faith and prove the sincerity of my love for my wonderful son.

About a year before my son repented, the Lord told me to stop exhorting him to go to church. He told me my son was enjoying our conversations so he would go just to please me out of obligation, not because his heart was ready. He must not go until the Lord had prepared the way for him. So, I told my son what the Lord said to me and he was relieved. All my cards were on the table for him to see. God's love was there to see, too.

Christ is both man and God. He knows what it is like to be both, the ultimate in empathy. The Word became flesh and dwelt among us. (John 1:14) My role as an intercessor requires identification with both the righteousness of Christ and the weakness of sinful man. In identifying with Christ, I must see myself as a new creation in Him, as being like the Lord in spirit. I must also confess any active sin and plead the Blood first for myself, that I may approach God in the Righteousness of Christ—that my prayers be not hindered. Then, I must claim verses like **Ephesians 2:4-10**, which declare that I am seated at the Right Hand of God in Christ Jesus, above all powers and principalities, which are under Christ's Feet. Because I am in Him, those powers are also under *my feet*. This is God's doing, not mine. Then, in the favor that Christ has from His Father, I stand in the place of my son, for whom I am interceding and say:

Lord, I plead the Blood for him also. I stand in his place in his behalf. You stood in mine and took the punishment I deserved, pleading mercy for me. Your grace enabled my eyes to be opened, my ears to hear, and my heart to understand, that I might repent. I pray for mercy that You will not give him the punishment his sins deserve, either.

I pray that his eyes will be opened, that his ears will be able to hear, and his heart will be able to understand, and that You will grant him the gift of repentance. Because You said what we bind on earth is bound in heaven, I bind the power of Satan and restrict his inter-ference. I bind my son to the will and love of God. Because You said that what we release on earth will be released in heaven, I release him from the bonds of deception that hold him. I pray Lord that You will release Your love, favor, and mercy on him as I lift him up to You. I commit him to You in Jesus' wonderful Name, amen!

Then I needed to *stand* on what I was trusting for, as I waited pa-tiently for the answer, being willing at all times to speak when the Spirit told me to, or be silent, to do as the Spirit told me to do, or to get out of the way. It's important to see intercession as action as well as words. Over the course of my stand, I must be prepared to fast, exhort, encourage, and rebuke when necessary. Sometimes when I'm asking God to say such and such to the one I'm praying for, He will say, "Go and say those words to him yourself—you are My instrument!" I must be willing to experience rejection, condem-nation, discouragement and false starts. I found it necessary to turn him over to the Lord for whatever consequences were necessary to bring about his repentance.

But remember, the one for whom you are praying has a free will and must come to a *willing* surrender. Only God knows what it will take and when it will happen. The Lord has proven repeatedly that He is a rewarder of those who seek Him. Now it is my joy to be in wonderful fellowship with my son, whom the Lord has delivered, and restored to faith, and restored to me.

The day finally came when my son said to me, "I was reading the Gospel of John last night." I asked him, "What did you see?" He said, "It was hard to understand, I haven't read the Bible in a long time." After a few days of continued reading he said, "Remember that church you told me about last year? I think I'm going to check it out this Sunday."

I excitedly waited to hear from him the following Monday. He called me and said he was going to go to that church and get involved. He said he had dumped his stash and deleted all contact info from his former friends, and was going to make new ones at this church. He was about twenty when he left home. At thirty-four, he was completely reconciled and rededicated himself to the Lord! We have had wonderful fellowship with each other ever since.

ASSIGNMENT

In your own words, write a practice letter of what you need to say to **one** person who really needs an amends from you, but don't send it yet. Once you get the hang of it, you can write letters to others, though a personal conversation is always best. Writing a letter first can help you think it through and make a more honest and sincere communication.

Write an amends letter to a person you know you need to, naming the **specific things** you know that person is angry about.

Take careful consideration of your tone and attitude in the EXAMPLE LETTER on **page 153**. Be sure to **Show Throat.**

10

The Maintenance Of Relationship

Father, help me know that I am changed, that I have a new nature—able to bear Your good fruit, because of Christ, and Your Holy Spirit union with me, in my spirit.

Sanctification Dream

I drew a razor over my flesh and harvested every hair I could reach with my own hand. I trimmed my nails and the lashes of my eyes, my nose and every orifice, then heaped them on a stone. I set it all alight and sat naked before the stinking twist of smoke that curled up to heaven.

My vanity was only quenched for a moment as I prostrated myself and prayed. "My sins sprout from me more bountifully than the hairs on my body, which are as natural for my soul to produce. If I had a razor to shave my heart, stubble would reappear momentarily. How shall I be holy as You Are? What meaning is there in repentance? What does it profit to cut myself to the quick, to be raw and sore with reproach, to be exhaustive in confession and the master of shame, but still be the slave of myself? How is it that I am dead to sin? Is not the shedding of the Blood for more purpose than just excusing me from my own life?"

After doing an inventory like this, you might share my despair in the futility of my own efforts at lasting repentance. On one occasion of exhausting confession, the Lord said to me, "You're being honest, but you're not speaking the truth!" I was honest about my sins, but my conclusions about God and myself were not true. I was not understanding what was possible in the Lord. And I was misbelieving that what my flesh wanted was what the real me wanted to do. Sadly, most churches only teach about being *excused* from our sins—some adding ritual absolution and penance as additional requirements. Exhortation to go and sin no more is right, but how was I to do that? Where was the Biblical foundation for the power of God to change me into an overcomer?

Luke 18:27 says:

> But He said, "What is impossible with man is possible with God." – ESV

Philippians 2:13 says,

> For it is God who worketh in you, both to **will** and to **do** of His good pleasure. – KJ21 (Shank)

True Self Versus False Self

But I didn't yet know that as long as I allowed myself to measure my spiritual progress by my flesh, I would be forever discouraged. My flesh *never* wants to do God's will. My flesh is hopeless, sold to sin **(Romans 7:14)**. It is irredeemably corrupted. Satan knows this. As long as he can keep me focused on trying to fix an unfixable problem, he will be able to keep me in futility and from seeing the truth.

John 15:1-6 says:

I am the true Vine, and My Father is the Vinedresser. Every branch in Me that does not bear fruit He takes away, and every branch that does bear fruit He prunes, that it may bear more fruit. Already you are clean because of the word that I have spoken to you. Abide **in** Me and I **in** you. As the branch cannot bear fruit by itself, unless it abides **in** the vine, neither can you unless you **abide in** Me. I am the Vine; you are the branches. Whoever **abides in** Me and I in him, he it is who bears much fruit, for apart from Me you can do nothing. If anyone does **not** abide in Me he is **thrown** away like a branch and withers; and the branches are gathered, thrown into the fire and burned. — ESV **(Shank)**

John 14:18-24 says:

I will not leave you as orphans; I will come to you. Yet a little while and the world will see Me no more, but you will see Me. Because I live, you also will live. In that day you will know that I am **in** My Father, and you **in** Me, and I **in** you. Whoever has My commandments and keeps them, he it is who loves Me. And he who loves Me will be loved by My

Father, and I will **manifest** Myself to him. Judas (not Iscariot) said to Him, Lord, how is it that You **manifest** Yourself to us, and not to the world? Jesus answered him, If anyone loves Me, he will keep My word, and My Father will love him, and We will come to him and **make Our home** with him. Whoever does not love Me does not keep My words. And the word that you hear is not Mine but the Father Who sent Me. — ESV (Shank)

Having been reconciled to God in Jesus Christ, I must maintain my relationship with Him in loving attention and devotion, by abiding in (**living in**) Him—that He may be **manifest in** me. I must seek Him in prayer and through careful study of His Word. I must praise Him with all my heart and express gratitude with thanksgiving. Gratitude is an attitude, not just a feeling. I must confess the truth about Him and hold Him blameless in character because the Lord is good. If I have a grievance against Him, I must speak it out as a respectful question because there are many things I do not understand about His ways. Why is this happening to me? Are You displeased with me? Is this from You or is it from the devil? I must listen for His answer as I wait. God is Holy.

I must bring my needs and the needs of others before Him trusting that He will answer my petitions, because He is a rewarder of those who have faith in Him. When His answer is yes, I must give Him thanks. When His answer is no, I must trust His way is right, however disappointing. My honest grieving must not turn to bitterness of heart. I must not give my heart to an idol I desire, or allow a root of bitterness to take hold.

I must confess the biblical truth about me—who I am in Christ. The truth about me must also include the confession of my sins against

Him, as well as my sins against others, to restore credibility to my being in Christ and He in me. I must humbly ask for forgiveness with a clear and fearless understanding of my offense, not minimizing it or making excuses. I must make a priority to make amends to those whom I have offended, with real remorse.

I must be quick to forgive those who have offended me because the Lord is always quick to forgive me. Revenge or consequences are for the Lord to determine, for me as much as for the one who has harmed me. When painful recall comes back from Satan to provoke me, I must rebuke him with the words that stand on my forgiving prayer: *God is my witness—I have forgiven this one who has hurt me! I refuse condemnation for the painful emotions I am re-experiencing. My emotions may be intense, but Christ through me no longer wants revenge.*

Forgiveness must always be given to those who offend me, but trust must be earned. My forgiveness does not mean I must stay in situations where I may be further abused if the offender is unwilling to change. Healthy boundaries are good if my offender will not change. But, I must love my enemy. This is why we must not be unequally yoked in marriage. If both parties believe, God can bring reconciliation where there is faith. As a last resort, divorce is permitted for unrepented adultery, abandonment and physical violence.

In my daily relationships, I must look for ways to build up and encourage others. Do I not feel encouraged when people praise or give credit to me? Those who excel in a skill or achievement should be praised, not envied. Those who show me kindness should be warmly thanked. Give honor to those in authority. When criticism is necessary, I must show kindness and humility. Is it not easier for me to receive criticism if I know I am loved by the one saying what needs to be said? I should grieve with those who grieve, rejoice with those who rejoice. I must love my neighbor as I love myself.

Romans 12:9-21 says:

> Let love be genuine. Abhor [hate] what is evil; hold fast to what is good. Love one another with brotherly affection. Outdo one another in showing honor. Do not be slothful [procrastinating] in zeal, be fervent [persistent] in spirit, serve the Lord. Rejoice in hope, be patient in tribulation, be constant in prayer. Contribute to the needs of the saints and seek to show hospitality.
>
> Bless those who persecute you; bless and do not curse them. Rejoice with those who rejoice, weep with those who weep. Live in harmony with one another. Do not be haughty [arrogant], but associate with the lowly. Never be wise in your own sight. Repay no one evil for evil but give thought to what is honorable in the sight of all. If possible, so far as it depends on you, live peaceably with all. Beloved, never avenge yourselves, but leave it to the wrath of God, for it is written, "Vengeance is Mine, I will repay, says the Lord." To the contrary, "if your enemy is hungry, feed him; if he is thirsty, give him something to drink; for by so doing you will heap burning coals [of conviction] on his head." Do not be overcome with evil but overcome evil with good. — ESV [Shank]

If I am grateful to someone, I should say thank you. If I can help someone, I should do so. If someone does something worthy of praise, I should give that person credit. If someone needs to know they are in the wrong, I should correct them in humility and respect.

As I judge, so shall I be judged. I should treat others as I wish to be treated whether I receive goodness from them or not.

1 Peter 2:21-25 says,

> For to this you have been called because Christ also suffered for you, leaving you an example, so that you might follow in His steps. He committed no sin, neither was deceit found in His Mouth. When He was reviled [cursed], He did not revile in return; when He suffered, He did not threaten, but continued trusting Himself to Him Who judges justly. He Himself bore our sins in His Body on the tree, that we might die to sin and live to righteousness. By His wounds, you have been healed. For you were straying like sheep but have now returned to the Shepherd and Overseer of your souls. — ESV [Shank]

Am I to do all these things in my own strength? No, I cannot. And I was never meant to. I was meant to be the container and the expression of Christ not myself. I am not just a sinner saved by grace. I am much more. My Savior is also my Keeper. I must believe that, by making choices *as if* the Word of God is true. I should not be led by how things look or feel. He that has the Spirit of God in one spirit with Him.

Overcoming vs. Being Overthrown

Matthew 17:19-20 says,

> Then the disciples came to Jesus privately and said, "Why could we not cast it out?"
>
> He said to them, "Because of your little faith. For truly I say to you, if you have faith like a grain of a mustard seed, you

will say to this mountain, 'Move from here to there,' and it will move, and nothing will be impossible for you." – ESV

The **logos**, the Word of God does not lie. It is not enough for me to give merely mental ascent to this statement. My heart must believe it also. So how do I make my heart believe?

Hebrews 4:1-2 says,
> Therefore, since the promise of entering His rest still stands, let us be careful that none of you be found to have fallen short of it. For we also have had the gospel preached to us, just as they [**Israel**] did; but the message [**logos**] they heard was of no value to them, because those who heard did not *combine* it with faith. (*the word was not **mixed with faith** in those who heard it*). – NIV (Shank)

Hebrews 4:6 says they failed to enter in because of *unbelief*, so they died in the wilderness. God swore an oath in righteous anger that they would not enter into His rest. It is true that faith comes first by hearing, but what is heard must produce the obedience of faith. This comes when we start making choices *as if* the Word is true— by mixing obedient action with what we have heard—to produce real faith.

Sin had made my life like a house with holes in its walls. In areas of greater weakness, I had larger holes for the enemy to reach in and steal from me. How can faith fill in these holes? Speaking the truth back to the enemy's lies is certainly a good start, but making a choice *as if* the Word of the Lord is true, has substance. My choice to *act as if* the Word is True, mixes my Maker's power with me to make a "brick" that I can lay in the hole in my wall. Inversely, if I mix my faith with a lie, *as if* the lie is true, I will widen the hole in my wall because the Unmaker's power destroys. As Norman Grubb says: *"what I take, takes me."* If I give in to temptation *sin takes me,* and I will bear the fruit of that sin till I repent. It has been wonderful to find out that when I obey the Lord, His *righteousness will take me* and I will once again bear His fruit.

Alas, much of the church teaches *only* about the Blood atonement through Jesus. But little is taught about the power of Christ in us to really change due to our spiritual union with Him. This can result in the problem of holding the form of godliness, but denying its power. **(1 Timothy 3:5)**

Galatians 2:20 says,

> I have been crucified with Christ. It is no longer I who live, but Christ Who lives in me. And the life I now live in the flesh I live by the faith of the Son **[tou uiou]** of God, Who loved me and gave Himself for me. – ESV [Shank]

Again, all the major translations except for the King James say, "I live by faith in the Son of God." Of course, we believe in Jesus, But the Greek says something stronger here, "I live by the faith of the Son of God..." *Jesus' faith is upholding my faith!*

Romans 6:5-6 says,

> For if we are united with Him in a death like His, we shall certainly be united with Him in a resurrection like His. We know that our old self was crucified with Him in order that the body of sin might be brought to nothing, so that we would no longer be enslaved to sin. For one who has died has been set free from sin. – ESV

How can this be? Again, as I stated the question before on page **81**, Jesus died 2000 years ago – there was not even an atom of me then.

How could I possibly have died with Him? Now I see it. When I was born again, God joined me to the One who died back then.

And **1 Corinthians 6:17** says:

> but he that has joined to the Lord becomes one spirit with Him.

Ephesians 5:28-33 says:

> In the same way husbands should love their wives as their own bodies. He who loves his wife loves himself. For no one ever hated his own flesh, but nourishes and cherishes it, just as Christ does the church, because we are members of his body. "Therefore a man shall leave his father and mother and hold fast to his wife, and the two shall become one flesh." This mystery is profound, and I am saying that it refers to Christ and the church. However, let each one of you love his wife as himself, and let the wife see that she respects her husband. – ESV

Christ is the Bridegroom. The Church is called the Bride. I believe the human spirit is female in the sense that it receives into itself the Spirit of God, like a bride receives her husband into herself when they marry. My union with Christ makes me godly. His Holy Spirit is in union with my human spirit. I am in union with His Holy Spirit. In this way the Bride of Christ (the Church) is one with Him. The Bride is joined to the Groom and receives all He has. And she is to give to Him all that she has. The Bride receives all that the Bridegroom has won for her. She is now holy from her union with Him. I am now holy because of my union with Him.

Ephesians 2:4 says,

> But God, being rich in mercy, because of the great love with which He loved us, even when we were dead in our trespasses, made us alive together with Christ—by grace you have been saved—and raised us up with Him in the heavenly places in Christ Jesus... – ESV

If Jesus is seated at the Right Hand of God, above all powers and principalities, so am I.

So, I have been betrayed by a friend who revealed painful confidences about me that I had once confessed to him in trust. Now my reputation is destroyed in the minds of all who heard it. The desire for revenge rises in me to betray confidences he shared about himself to me, in retaliation. His wound can widen the hole made by other wounds that Satan has used to gain access to me through bitterness and revenge. But the Word of the Lord that *does not lie* says, "you shall not return evil for evil, but return good for evil." So, I must make a choice to *mix faith with the Word* by not slandering in return.

Will the emotions of my soul shake with rage? Yes. Will my mind not obsess with terrible scenarios of spreading damage and consequences back on him? **Yes.** But my spirit must speak back to my soul with the truth that God will vindicate me in this life or the next, because I have obeyed His Word. When I do that, the *righteousness* of the Word that does not lie *will take me.* My soul will then be able to start to calm down. Depending on the size of the wound and how deeply my revenge habit is engrained, I will experience withdrawal from my old ways. But withdrawal is survivable. It will not last forever.

There is a limit to what I must endure, but through more temptation, I have more opportunities to make choices to act *as if* the Lord is keeping me. And because He is holding me, I can make more faith bricks to fill up the hole made by the bitterness of past wounds. Bricks are made by *mixing my faith with the Word*—by taking righteous obedient action. As my own holes start to fill in, I can also continue to produce more bricks to add onto the house of my life, making other rooms to minister to the weak and the lost with prayers and deeds of faith on their behalf. The prayers of the righteous avail much.

This is not "fake it till you make it." *Faking it* implies what I stand on may not really have substance, or that by the force of my own will I can make something appear to be true for which I have no basis. But who am I? I am a branch snatched away from the fire— now grafted into the Vine of Christ. I am now one spirit with Him Who gave me His Spirit, that I may enter into His rest and bear His fruit! ...He who is joined to the Lord is one spirit with Him. (**1 Corinthians 6:17**)

Galatians 5:22-25 says:
> But the fruit of the Spirit is love, joy, peace, patience, kindness, goodness, faithfulness, gentleness, selfcontrol; against such things there is no law. And those who belong to Christ Jesus have crucified the flesh with its passions and desires. If we live by the Spirit, let us also keep in step with the Spirit. - ESV

2 Peter 1:4 says:
> ... by which he has granted to us his precious and very great promises, so that through them you may become *partakers*

of the divine nature, having escaped from the corruption that is in the world because of sinful desire. – ESV (*Shank*)

The more I recover from my shame-based responses to my environment and circumstances, the more liberty I will enjoy in Christ.

My handicaps do not give me an excuse for not exercising faith. My special circumstances are no excuse for faithlessness, either. I am to be defined by Christ-in-me, and nothing less—that I may overcome by the Overcomer in me. I AM FREE!

John 8:36 says:
> So if the Son sets you free, you will be free indeed.

THE FREEDOMS

Freedom to Listen
I can suspend the prejudice of my opinion to hear what another has to say. If they are right about what they say, I have gained wisdom. If they are mistaken, my position can be retaken with greater confidence.

Freedom from Blame
I will no longer have to seek a scapegoat for my problems. I will be free to do whatever needs to be done to fix them, with the grace to learn from mistakes—yours or mine.

Freedom from Control
I will no longer have to make rules for others to follow. My behavior boundaries are for me to follow—not you.

Freedom to be Honest

I will no longer have to cover myself with excuses, lies, or use flat-tery or half-truths to mislead you. I can be real. I will no longer be a slave to the opinions of others about my value or worth.

Freedom to Know Truth

I will be able to learn from anyone. It will no longer be about *who* is right—me or you. It will be more about *what* is right—this or that. I am not the subject, the truth, is.

Freedom from Condemnation

I will no longer have to beat myself up. Having no expectations of perfection for myself in my flesh, I will no longer have to impose those expectations on you or me. I am forgiven.

Freedom to Love

I will no longer have to be imprisoned by guilt or revenge. I will experience healing in my heart by forgiving others, and help others to heal by making amends to them for the wrongs I have done. I will become an instrument in restoring broken relationships. I will have freedom to give without being obligated.

Freedom to stand before God in Confidence

I will be able to enjoy my Lord in worship and prayer. I will be able to pray for others with confident expectation of an answer. I will be able to hear the Voice of the Lord when He speaks to me.

In Conclusion

To you who have completed the hard work of **looking** where you did not want to look, **seeing** what you did not want to see, **feeling** what you did not want to feel, and even **knowing** what you might not have wanted to know about yourself—BE BLESSED!

I pray you may now see and believe more of the truth, as you learn to exchange your old sinful ways for the wonderful ways which are yours in the Vine of Christ Jesus. You have freedom from the **Root of Shame**. Humbly seek the Lord for deeper healing. Continue to be brave in facing whatever the Holy Spirit shows you to work on. Do not grieve the Spirit by closing your heart to His conviction. That will create more shame.

He wants to give you deeper revelation as to Who Christ really is and who you really are in Him. The largely undiscovered self that God has made you to be as His child, is made for both you and God to enjoy together, forever. Let us press on in that wonderful discovery, in Jesus' Name. Amen.

Isaiah 61:1–7 is a Messianic prophecy where Jesus says:

> The Spirit of the Sovereign Lord is on Me,
> because the Lord has anointed Me
> to proclaim good news to the poor.
> He has sent Me to bind up the brokenhearted,
> to proclaim freedom for the captives
> and release from darkness for the prisoners,
> to proclaim the year of the Lord's favor
> and the day of vengeance of our God,
> to comfort all who mourn,
> and provide for those who grieve in Zion—
> to bestow on them a crown of beauty
> instead of ashes,

the oil of joy
instead of mourning,
and a garment of praise
instead of a spirit of despair.
They will be called oaks of righteousness,
a planting of the Lord
for the display of His splendor.
They will rebuild the ancient ruins
and restore the places long devastated;
they will renew the ruined cities
that have been devastated for generations.
Strangers will shepherd your flocks;
foreigners will work your fields and vineyards.
And you will be called priests of the Lord,
you will be named ministers of our God.
You will feed on the wealth of nations,
and in their riches you will boast.
Instead of your **shame**
you will receive a double portion,
and instead of **disgrace**
you will rejoice in your inheritance.
And so you will inherit a double portion in your land,
and everlasting joy will be yours. – NIV (**Shank**)

Epilogue

A Guide to Discussion Group Leaders

It is important that those who will lead or teach this book be transparent. By all means lead the readings and discussions for the sake of order, but avoid academic distance from this subject. Reading the chapters aloud in class time is a good idea. That duty can be shared. Questions will arise. These can be discussed openly so all can be on the same page of understanding. This approach to each chapter makes more productive processing on the chart homework between classes. I allow about 60-90 minutes for each class.

Talking about your own personal struggles with shame make it easier for the other participants to be transparent. The more they feel free to volunteer intimate information about themselves, the more unified the group will become. There are many examples of sinful traits in each chapter. If you can identify with some of them, make admissions and comment on them. Your example of courage will give courage to the others.

There are two critical areas of this book which require concentrated attention. The first is the **Trigger Loop and Loop Breaker** sentences at the end of **Chapter 6**. Many people have difficulty in trying to construct them at first. This is often because they have not been keeping up with their chart assignments, or have made poor reasoning interpretations. When all the columns are filled in, repeated behavior patterns may then be easily observed. The Trigger Loop examples given from pages 103 – 110 can also help in how to see patterns that can be modified to fit their own.

Those unaccustomed to analytical thinking may also struggle and ask for help. Good. The emotionally dishonest might need to be challenged. Also good. Those who refuse to keep up with their charts should be encouraged to start over next time.

I have found it helpful to spend 2-3 sessions on the **Chapter 6** sentences, until they all catch on. I recommend asking each member of the class to share their process findings. They should fill in the blanks in pencil because there are sure to be refinements and corrections as more insight comes—pens will make changes messy. Those who catch on quickly are encouraged to help the others. The samples provided in the chapter can prove helpful for clues in how to think this process through. Hopefully, the group will have established enough trust with each other by this time to make it exciting. Those who are clueless at first may be a little embarrassed, but making it exciting to discover hidden conceits and agendas can be very stimulating.

Listen carefully to each part of the sequence as they read their sentences. Take notes. Questioning the interpreter is easy, but often the **conceit** and the false *payoff* agenda are not clear. Be helpful and encouraging to them. The goal of this exercise is to develop a new skill so they can spot what Satan is up to in their process. Your skills will also improve as you help others. Jesus says we should be innocent as doves (not naive) but wise as serpents. The wisdom we are pursuing here is learning how the serpent has had his way with us in the past, so he will not so easily fool us again. Deeper repentance in our motives and agendas can bring deeper healing, too.

The second area needing concentrated attention is the amends letter in **Chapter 9**. The purpose of this exercise is also to develop a skill.

Some may have high anxiety about approaching someone they have harmed because the other person has harmed them as well—or that person may still be very angry. Encourage them *but do not push them*. Concentrate on getting the draft right for now. The Holy Spirit will show when the time is right to act.

Pointing out the potential for insult in the way the letter is worded, can help prevent sabotage. Blame and excuses must be removed. Humility and empathy must be encouraged.

These things must be approached in steps. I may not be ready or willing to make an amends yet. But in writing a letter I am **not forced to send,** I can help prepare my mind and heart for when the time is right. Why should I look so hard at my sins and motives when the person I have offended seems to have no desire to look at their offences to me? The answer is so God can heal me and make me an instrument in healing others. This exercise is valid even if the one I need to make amends to is now dead. In such cases, I can share my letter with the group, then burn it in solemnity.

One To One Follow Ups

Meeting with each participant after the classes are finished can be extremely helpful. Questions and problems with homework that still remain can be cleared up. But even more important is the spiritual condition of each student. The power for real change comes from our spiritual union with the Holy Spirit's indwelling. Being born again. The leverage in this book for real change comes from the power in being a whole new person in Christ. Anything less will have limited results at best.

- An unbeliever *does not* have the power of the Holy Spirit.

- Some people believe they are Christians just because they mentally agree that Jesus died for their sins. Or they were raised in church but have not really given themselves to the Lord. They are only *culturally* Christian in their beliefs. These also *lack the power* of the Spirit, to change.

- Those who are real believers but have not been taught what being in Christ—and Christ being in them—really means, may have no experiential knowledge of this power. So faith for that person may be about little more than being *excused* for sinning, not learning how to overcome besetting weaknesses by the power of the Holy Spirit. So shame remains through ignorance or a lack of moral integrity.

For this reason, revisiting the **House Cleaning Prayer** in **Chapter 2** on page **43** can make a real difference as a diagnostic tool for what a person really believes. As a teacher or leader, you, yourself may

need to make sure you are clear on all these points, and can say so with your own lips. You can download extra copies of this prayer from:
johnbyronshank.com/Books/Free Downloads/House Cleaning Prayer/Get it

Read carefully through the prayer with each one privately. Wherever they have questions, help them understand. If they are not ready to pray **do not push them**. Real faith requires a free will choice. It is better to wait till their hearts are ready to believe. Otherwise, when thinking they are in Jesus, they find they have no real intimate connection with Him. Or they may find they have no real power to obey, and then dismiss real faith altogether.

House Cleaning Prayer (from page 43)

> Father God in heaven, I believe Jesus is Your only begotten Son, Who was born in the flesh like me, was tempted in every way as I am, but without sinning, and that He suffered and died in my place to pay for all my sin. Then He rose from the dead and is now seated at Your Right Hand, in heaven.

Jesus says no one comes to the Father except by Me. If the one you are praying with does not accept the words above after you have explained them, **STOP**. They are not yet ready.

> I freely confess to being a sinner who desperately needs the Blood of Jesus to be saved. I agree with You Lord, that I am guilty of all the sins Your Holy Spirit has shown me to be wrong.

Reluctance to acknowledge known sin, once you have explained why, this a another good reason to **STOP**.

I renounce Satan and all his works in my life, and I turn away from him to serve my new Master, the Lord Jesus Christ.

I renounce the lies from Satan that I have believed, as the Holy Spirit reveals those lies to me.

I renounce my bitterness and rights to revenge, which I have held against You, Lord, and those who have harmed me.

I renounce my fears that Satan has used to cause me to suppress my conscience, steal my boldness, and withhold love from You and those around me.

I renounce my shame that Satan has used to make me a liar, a deceiver, and one who tries to hide from Your Goodness, O Lord.

Hesitancy to renounce Satan in any of these areas after you have explained why, is good reason to **STOP**.

Father, I do not deserve Your mercy, but please be merciful to me and forgive me all my sins, because of what Your Righteous Son has done in love for me. Teach me what You are really like by showing me Your Truth and Your lovingkindness.

Any lack of humility or unwillingness which does not go away when you have pointed it out, is a good reason to **STOP**.

Please fill me with Your Holy Spirit that I may be born again as a new creation in Christ, with *the power to repent and follow* You faithfully, and to bear Your fruit of righteousness in my life.

If the person you are praying with says being born again is not from their spiritual tradition, explain what Jesus says to Nicodemus in **John 3:1-6**, or what Jesus says about the Vine and branches in **John 15:1-11**. If they remain unpersuaded, **STOP**.

> Open Your Word to me that I may learn Your living wisdom.
>
> Heal my bitterness as I learn to forgive those who harm me, that I may become sweet.
>
> May Your Word fill me with faith to face all my fears with righteous courage and help me to be quick to confess and repent when I have sinned.
>
> Please clothe the nakedness of my shame. And please deliver me from habits of willful disobedience.
>
> Receive me now into Your keeping and lead me to a strong Bible believing church where I may be baptized and become a disciple.

I share the frustration that a strong Bible believing church can be hard to find, but the request that the Lord lead me to one that I may submit, is the point. Unwillingness to be led is reason to **STOP**.

> I thank You Lord and trust that You will give me the grace I need for my weaknesses, so I may be able to follow You faithfully, in Jesus' Wonderful Name, amen.

If we must **STOP** the prayer reading because we perceive the person is not ready, we can still respectfully encourage them to consider the stopping points they have in themselves, and ask the Lord to help them see what must be seen and know what must be known. Only then should the benediction below be given.

If they are ready to pray the prayer above, give them these words of blessing afterwards, because they have believed: *(You should ask for permission to lay your hand on their shoulder and pray these words over them.)*

> May the Lord anoint you with His Holy Spirit because you have believed in your heart and have confessed with your lips that Jesus is Lord. May His Spirit fill you and lift your spirit with the power to overcome evil. May the eyes of your heart be opened to His Wonders and His Lovingkindness. May He open His Word to you with wisdom and understanding. And may the Lord refresh you, heal you, and keep you in Jesus' Wonderful Name, amen!

I make copies of this prayer so it can be signed and dated, making myself a witness. This copy may be kept by each for encouragement.

Bibliography

THE HOLY BIBLE by **The Holy Spirit** *(Primarily ESV Translation)*
/ Crossway Bibles, Good News Publishers

The Revised Standard Version (RSV) / A. J. Holman Co.

The New International Version (NIV) / AMG Publishers

King James Version (KJV) / AMG Publishers

Expository Dictionary of New Testament Words / **W. E. Vine** / Revel

Outline Studies in Christian Doctrine / **Rev. George Pardington, PhD.** / Christian Publications Inc.

Yes I Am by **Norman Grubb** / Overcomer Literature Trust, Zerubbabel Press

Narcissism, Denial of the True Self / **Alexander Lowen, MD** / Collier Books

Healing The Wounded Heart, The Heartache of Sexual Abuse and Hope of Transformation / **Dan B. Allender** / BakerBooks

War on the Saints (Unabridged version) / **Jesse Penn-Lewis** / Howe

Excerpts from *Deep Discipling* / **John Byron Shank** / Peniel Publishing / Amazon.com

Recovering My Integrity as a Father / **John Byron Shank** / Peniel Publishing

Alcoholics Anonymous / AA World Services

Games People Play by **Eric Berne, M.D.** / Ballantine Books

SECRET SERMONS / **Victoria Hope Peterson** / Amazon.com

Inspired sermons and conversations / **many friends and teachers**

The School of Hard Knocks / **The Holy Spirit**

BibleGateway.com